Set
APART
for
GOD

Set
APART
for
GOD

Derek PRINCE

WHITAKER
HOUSE

Publisher's Note: This book was compiled from the extensive archive of Derek Prince's unpublished materials and edited by the Derek Prince Ministries editorial team.

All Hebrew and Greek definitions are the author's, with the exception of *charitoo*. See *Strong's Exhaustive Concordance of the Bible*, #G5487.

SET APART FOR GOD
The Beautiful Secret of Holiness

Derek Prince Ministries
P.O. Box 19501
Charlotte, North Carolina 28219
www.derekprince.org

ISBN: 978-1-60374-288-7
Printed in the United States of America
© 2011 by Derek Prince Ministries–International

Whitaker House
1030 Hunt Valley Circle
New Kensington, PA 15068
www.whitakerhouse.com

Library of Congress Cataloging-in-Publication Data

Prince, Derek.
  Set apart for God : the beautiful secret of holiness / Derek Prince.
    p. cm.
  Summary: "Rather than being a list of rules, holiness means partaking of the divine nature through a relationship with the God who loves us, and fulfilling His call upon our lives"—Provided by publisher.
  ISBN 978-1-60374-288-7 (trade pbk. : alk. paper) 1. Holiness—Christianity. 2. Christian life—Pentecostal authors. I. Title.
  BT767.P79 2011
  234'.8—dc23
                                    2011027460

1 2 3 4 5 6 7 8 9 10 11 **W** 18 17 16 15 14 13 12 11

CONTENTS

FOREWORD

Before you begin *Set Apart for God: The Beautiful Secret of Holiness* by Derek Prince, may we offer some helpful remarks? Here are a few comments regarding the topic of the book you are about to read, as well as the process involved in placing it in your hands.

First, the topic. We trust you will be encouraged by the positive perspective Derek brings to this formerly abused and neglected topic. It probably will come as no surprise to you that not everyone is eager to pick up a book on the subject of "holiness." To the contrary, the instinctive reaction of many may be to avoid the topic altogether—either because they perceive it as outright religiosity or because they feel it too demanding a topic, or simply because the prospect of living a holy life seems utterly unattainable. (So, why even try?)

Such reactions are entirely understandable. In many ways, they represent some of the reasons this book has been so long in coming.

Holiness is a concept that for years has been distorted in the church and in Christian thought and practice. In fact, as Derek himself observes in this book, most Christians erroneously regard the pursuit of holy living as a strict adherence to a list of rules—mostly negative (a list of "don'ts")—that must be rigidly observed for a person to "measure up" in God's sight.

Refreshingly, Derek dispels that misconception and replaces it with an entirely different approach to holy living as an expression of our relationship with the Lord. He tells you not only what holiness is not, but also what it really ought to be.

Here is just a quick preview to entice you to dig deep into this book as you pursue your own goal to be set apart for God and to discover "the beautiful secret of holiness." Derek made this amazing statement: "It [holiness] is not just following a set of negative rules. It is a positive, powerful force. In fact, I believe that holiness is the most powerful force at work in the universe."

Second, the process. People regularly ask how it is possible to continue releasing "new" books by Derek Prince in the years following his passing. (As you may know, Derek passed away on September 24, 2003, after a sixty-year ministry of teaching the Word of God worldwide.)

Perhaps that same question has come to your mind. If so, let us offer a brief glimpse of our process in releasing new material. You may have noticed the explanatory statement at the beginning of each book: "Editor's note: This book was compiled from the extensive archives of Derek Prince's unpublished materials and edited by the Derek Prince Ministries Editorial Team."

Amazingly, the archives are full to overflowing with audio messages from Derek's prolific biblical teaching ministry. Many of these messages are even more pertinent and relevant to our time than to the period in which they were originally delivered. Consequently, we feel a heightened sense of urgency to make them available in printed form to the body of Christ.

The editorial team, with representatives from DPM offices in various parts of the world, regularly discusses what materials should be prepared for publication. Always in view is the fact that the work will subsequently be translated for distribution throughout many nations of the world.

In the case of this material, the international DPM community has long been hoping for the publication of a book by Derek Prince on holiness. For many years, he himself had intended to write the book, for it was a theme that was near and dear to his heart. However, works on other important topics kept moving ahead of this book on Derek's list of publishing priorities.

Discussions concerning the release of a book on holy living continued after Derek's passing, with the realistic recognition that a substantive book on this demanding theme may not get the hoped-for positive reception (for all the reasons cited earlier). The concern was that few Christians would seriously consider picking up a book on holiness.

Derek himself had not shared that concern. His opinion, often expressed (which could well have ended up the title of the book), was as follows: *Holiness Is Not an Option*. (As you may realize, Derek was never one to mince words.) In the end, we took the plunge not only on the topic, but also in the use of the word *holiness* in the subtitle—incorporating a phrase Derek coined: "The Beautiful Secret of Holiness."

With that background, we place before you this definitive work by Derek Prince, *Set Apart for God: The Beautiful Secret of Holiness*.

We hope you will not put this book down until you have discovered this beautiful secret for yourself. May God use Derek's words to help you realize how significantly you have been "set apart for God" for these challenging, history-making times. May God inspire you through these words to impact the world around you as a present-day follower of the Holy One Himself—our Lord Jesus Christ.

—The Editorial Team of Derek Prince Ministries

INTRODUCTION

Holiness is one of the great and unique themes of the Scriptures. No other book in the world reveals the nature of holiness as does the Bible. However, this topic has been neglected among many groups of God's people for some time, so that there has been relatively little teaching on it.

In Pursuit of Holiness

At one point in my ministry, I was preparing to give a series of messages entitled "In Pursuit of Holiness," taken from Hebrews 12:14: *"Pursue peace with all people, and holiness, without which no one will see the Lord."* In the process of my preparation, I reflected back over the years. At that time, I had been a preacher for more than fifty years, and I counted over forty-nine different nations in which I had preached to people from all kinds of denominational and ethnic backgrounds—about as wide a variety of people as you could imagine. Sadly, I could not recall ever having been among a group of people who appeared to be pursuing true holiness.

Maybe my memory was at fault. Or maybe I misjudged the people. But I could not recall ever having been in a congregation or other group of people of whom I could say with certainty that they were seeking holiness.

Holiness Has Disappeared from Our Christian Vocabulary

My impression is that about the time of World War I, certain subjects just dropped out of the thinking of Western Christians and were never really regained. One of those subjects was holiness. In fact, the word *holiness* seemed to disappear from the Christian vocabulary (along with certain other words, such as *sacrifice* and *self-denial*). The result of such neglect is always disastrous to God's people because, as we will see, holiness is the essence of what God is and what we are to be. *"As He who called you is holy, you also be holy in all your conduct, because it is written, 'Be holy, for I am holy'"* (1 Peter 1:15–16).

There are, of course, some groups within the total body of Christ that have denominational titles linked with the word *holiness*. Yet, I have observed that, in many cases, the presentation of holiness by such groups has been essentially a list of rules that have to be observed, and, often, there is very little scriptural basis offered for these rules.

God is holy, but not because He has a set of rules that He follows. Following a set of rules will not make you holy, either— even if they are good rules. You may decide to follow them. But, again, that is not what makes you holy. My personal conclusion is that holiness has almost nothing whatsoever to do with observing rules and regulations. It has to do with *partaking of the divine nature* through Christ by entering into a relationship with the God who loves us, discovering what He has called us to do, and fulfilling that call upon our lives. I trust that this truth will become clear to you as you read *Set Apart for God: The Beautiful Secret of Holiness.*

1

WHAT IS HOLINESS?

To begin to answer the essential question of "What is holiness?" let me first tell you what it is *not*. Understanding what holiness is not is a very important step in coming to know what it is, because many Christians have the same incorrect idea about holiness that I mentioned in the introduction to this book—basically, that holiness is a set of rules about where you may go, what you may eat, and how you may dress. Traditionally, at least in Great Britain and America, this has been many people's picture of holiness. Yet the apostle Paul was emphatic about the fact that subjecting yourself to regulations has nothing to do with holiness. In Colossians 2, he wrote,

> *Therefore, if you died with Christ from the basic principles of the world, why, as though living in the world, do you subject yourselves to regulations; "Do not touch, do not taste, do not handle," which all concern things which perish with the using; according to the commandments and doctrines of men? These things indeed have an appearance of wisdom in self-imposed religion, false humility, and neglect of the body, but are of no value against the indulgence of the flesh.*
>
> (verses 20–23)

What Paul stated in the above Scripture is profoundly true. The more you focus on what you must not do, the more power those activities have over you. They *"are of no value against the indulgence of the flesh."* You say to yourself, "I must not lose my temper, I must not lose my temper, I must not lose my temper." What is the next thing you do? You lose your temper. Why? Because you are focusing on the wrong thing.

Frankly, exhibiting a belief that holiness means rules and regulations turns other people off. "If that's holiness," they say, "I don't want to have anything to do with it."

Let me prove to you that a list of "don'ts" is not the holiness the Bible describes. Let's look first at Hebrews 12:10, which speaks about the discipline of God the Father as He deals with His children:

> **A list of "don'ts" is not the holiness the Bible describes.**

For they [our human fathers] *indeed for a few days chastened us as seemed best to them, but He* [God] *for our profit, that we may be partakers of His holiness.*

It is clear that rules are not the definition of biblical or divine holiness. Again, God is holy, but not because of a set of rules He establishes to check His own conduct. The discipline spoken of in the above verse has to do with partaking of God's nature through a relationship with Him.

Holiness Is the Unparalleled Aspect of God's Nature

Through the ages, preachers and theologians have offered many interpretations and definitions of holiness. Let me start right off with my simple definition: *Holiness is the unique aspect of God's nature that is without parallel anywhere else in the universe.*

In the Bible, we find many different aspects of the nature of God. We are told that God is wise. He is knowing. He is just. He is powerful. He is loving. Clearly, we see these attributes of God's nature: wisdom, knowledge, justice, power, and love. In the world around us, we can see examples that portray these characteristics in some way. We see people whom we esteem to be wise. We see people who obviously have a high degree of knowledge. We see aspects of justice. We recognize the concept of power. And, in some measure, we are all familiar with love.

The same is not true, however, when it comes to holiness. There is nothing on the human plane, outside of God and the people of God, that has any claim to the title "holy." The holiness of God is unique.

Therefore, in order to understand holiness, you have to know God. A person who does not know God has no concept whatsoever of holiness. This is one good way to distinguish between people who know God and people who do not know Him. You cannot distinguish them by their denominational titles. You cannot always distinguish them by the kind of language they use, because some people are professional religionists who use all the "correct" religious phrases. But when you find someone who has a conception of holiness, you find someone who has met God—because without God, there is no holiness.

The entire thirtieth chapter of Proverbs is a rather strange prophecy by a man named Agur. We know nothing about Agur other than what is told about him in that chapter. But, in the following verses, Agur said this of himself:

> *Surely I am more brutish than any man, and have not the understanding of a man. I neither learned wisdom, nor have the knowledge of the holy ["Holy One" NKJV].*
> (Proverbs 30:2–3 KJV)

You see, *"the knowledge of the holy"*—that is, the knowledge of God, the Holy One—is essential to knowing holiness. No matter how educated or cultivated a person may be, without the knowledge of the holy, in some sense, he is just an animal. He is brutish.

Agur said of himself, in essence, "I'm just living on the animal plane." It is really the revelation of the holiness of God that lifts man onto a higher plane than the animals.

Holiness Is the Essence of God

Let me suggest for your consideration that holiness is the essence of what God is, and what *only* God is. There is no one else who is holy but God. *"For You alone are holy"* (Revelation 15:4). No one and nothing else is holy. In addition, *everything* about God is holy. So, again, in order to have any kind of understanding of holiness, we have to have an understanding of God: who He is and what He is like.

In the sections that follow, I am going to give you an overview of God's attributes. It works out that there are seven general attributes, and that satisfies me and reassures me that I am on the right path, because seven is the number of perfection in the Bible. I believe holiness is the summation of all God's attributes.

> **Holiness is the summation of all God's attributes.**

In a sense, holiness cannot really be explained or defined in the way most other concepts can. It can only be revealed. There is no other way by which we can come to understand holiness except by direct revelation from God. (See 1 Corinthians 2:9–12.)

Seven Attributes of God

1. Light
2. Love

We will begin by looking at the first two attributes, light and love. God is light. In 1 John 1:5, John said,

> *This is the message which we have heard from Him and declare to you, that God is light and in Him is no darkness at all.*

It is not merely that God created light or sends forth light. He Himself *is* light.

Further on in the same epistle, we see the next attribute of God:

> *He who does not love does not know God, for God is love....And we have known and believed the love that God has for us. God is love, and he who abides in love abides in God, and God in him.* (1 John 4:8, 16)

God is both light and love. John Wesley's suggested definition of holiness was "perfect love." That is a wonderful thought, but I don't believe it is adequate as a definition. God is both light and love.

We also recognize that there is, as it were, a tension between light and love. As a vehicle for exposing your inadequacies and faults, light scares you; love, however, attracts you. We see this same tension in our relationship with God. We want to come close to Him, but we do not always feel able to face the light of His truth.

3. Justice/Judgment

God is also a God of justice and judgment. These related traits are absolutely part of His nature. In the Song of Moses in Deuteronomy 32, Moses emphasized God's justice:

> *For I proclaim the name of the LORD: ascribe greatness to our God. He is the Rock, His work is perfect; for all His ways are justice, a God of truth and without injustice; righteous and upright is He.* (verses 3–4)

Many people often accuse God of injustice in their own situations or circumstances. But the Bible says that there is no injustice in God. He is totally just; He is a God of truth and justice. I often refer to the words of Abraham in Genesis 18, when he was pleading with the Lord about Sodom:

> *Far be it from You to do such a thing as this, to slay the righteous with the wicked, so that the righteous*

should be as the wicked; far be it from You! Shall not the Judge of all the earth do right? (Genesis 18:25)

That is who God is. He is the Judge of all the earth, and He always does what is right. There is no injustice, no iniquity, with Him. We are sometimes tempted to believe that God is unjust, but the Scriptures state emphatically that such a belief is erroneous.

4. Anger/Wrath

The next attribute of God is represented by two related nouns—anger and wrath. Contemporary Christianity hardly makes room for these characteristics of God, but they are very important. God is a God of anger and wrath. The first chapter of the book of Nahum is really a remarkable presentation of this truth. It begins in an abrupt way, with very little in the way of a polite introduction.

God is jealous, and the LORD avenges; the LORD avenges and is furious. The LORD will take vengeance on His adversaries, and He reserves wrath for His enemies.
(verse 2)

There we have it. The Lord is angry, He is furious, and He avenges Himself. It is part of His divine, eternal nature. Frankly, if we leave that part out, we are not presenting a true picture of God. Today, the contemporary attitude is, "Well, if God should judge someone or something, at least He has to get our approval before He does it." That is not so. Those who think that way are in for a rude awakening.

We find information similar to the above Scripture in a passage from Revelation 14 that describes God's judgment on the Antichrist, or the Beast, and those who follow him:

Then a third angel followed them, saying with a loud voice, "If anyone worships the beast and his image, and receives his mark on his forehead or on his hand, he

*himself shall also drink of the wine of the wrath of God,
which is poured out full strength into the cup of His in-
dignation. He shall be tormented with fire and brimstone
in the presence of the holy angels and in the presence of
the Lamb. And the smoke of their torment ascends forever and ever; and they have no rest day or night, who
worship the beast and his image, and whoever receives
the mark of his name."* (Revelation 14:9–11)

Please notice that these violators will be tormented in the
presence of the Lamb. This image does not fit the contemporary
picture of "gentle Jesus, meek and mild." But the anger and
wrath described above are part of His divine, eternal character.
He is a judge.

In this respect, I think about the apostle John. At the Last
Supper, he reclined with his head on the chest of Jesus, and
he asked Him who it was who would betray Him. (See John
13:21–25.) John drew very close to Jesus in that setting. But
in Revelation 1, when John had a vision of Jesus as the Judge,
he *"fell at His feet as dead"* (verse 17). You see, there are many
sides to the character and personality of God and of Jesus.
Judgment and wrath are part of His eternal nature. What's
more, the judgment that He administers is eternal: *"They will
be tormented day and night forever and ever"* (Revelation 20:10).

There is currently in circulation a theory that God is too mer-
ciful ever to impose eternal punishment on anybody. According
to that erroneous view, even if people don't get reconciled with
Him, they will not ultimately be punished. That is simply not
scriptural. In fact, it is untrue. Furthermore, it is a very dangerous belief. I would never entertain such a thought, especially
because of what is written at the end of the book of Revelation.
This passage is right near the conclusion of the last chapter of
the book just before the final two verses. The Lord says,

*For I testify to everyone who hears the words of the
prophecy of this book: If anyone adds to these things,*

God will add to him the plagues that are written in this book; and if anyone takes away from the words of the book of this prophecy, God shall take away his part from the Book of Life, from the holy city, and from the things which are written in this book.

(Revelation 22:18–19)

If anything is clearly written in this book of Revelation, it is that eternal judgment is a reality. Far be it from me to take that truth away. I would not want my name to be taken away from the Book of Life.

This is a very important issue for us today. The philosophy of "humanism" is so self-righteous—actually sloppy, I would say. It does not present an accurate picture of the way things are.

I had always thought of humanism as a comparatively harmless error. When I consulted a dictionary, however, I was taken aback by its definition:

the denial of any power or moral value superior to that of humanity; the rejection of religion in favor of a belief in the advancement of humanity by its own efforts.

I realized that humanism is not spiritually neutral. On the contrary, it is a deliberate denial and rejection of God's power and authority. It is an anti-religious philosophy. For this reason, it can be—and often is—taught in educational systems, such as that of the U.S.A., which prohibit the teaching of religion in its usual sense.

In fact, the sloppiness of humanistic thought has brought us to a stage in our society where the criminal is treated more kindly than the victim. Why? We don't want to be "judgmental."

Why don't we want to be judgmental? Here is my opinion: Secretly, we know in our hearts that if there is judgment for that other person, then there is also judgment for us. Since I don't want judgment on him (and therefore upon me), I'll arrange my view of God accordingly. But God doesn't play that game.

5. Mercy/Lovingkindness

Another great attribute of God is represented by the related words: mercy and lovingkindness. The Hebrew word *chesed* is translated into English as "lovingkindness" in the *New King James Version*, though it is not always translated in that way in other Bible versions. For example, it has been translated as *"great love"* (NIV) and *"steadfast love"* (RSV). As I have studied the word *chesed*, I've come to the conclusion that what it really means is "the covenant-keeping faithfulness of God." God's faithfulness to His covenant is one of His great attributes.

> **God's faithfulness to His covenant is one of His great attributes.**

Psalm 51 is a prayer of David. It was prayed, as you may know, in a time of deep distress, when his soul was hanging in the balance after his sins of committing adultery with Bathsheba and murdering her husband, Uriah, had been uncovered. We can thank God that David knew to whom to pray and on what basis to pray; it helps us in our own understanding of God's lovingkindness. This is David's prayer of repentance:

> *Have mercy upon me, O God, according to Your lovingkindness; according to the multitude of Your tender mercies, blot out my transgressions.*   (Psalm 51:1)

"According to Your lovingkindness" means "according to Your covenant-keeping faithfulness." David was saying to the Lord, "You've committed Yourself to forgive me, if I meet the conditions. I'm appealing to You on that basis." How important it is for us to be able to approach God on that basis.

The same principle can be found in various other psalms, such as in the first verse of Psalm 106:

Praise the LORD! Oh, give thanks to the LORD, for He is good! For His mercy [chesed: His lovingkindness, His faithfulness to His covenant] endures forever.

In Psalm 107, the above statement of thanks for God's mercy occurs again: *"Oh, give thanks to the LORD, for He is good! For His mercy [chesed] endures forever"* (verse 1). In addition, the word *chesed* occurs in the following repeated exclamation, which appears four times in this psalm:

Oh, that men would give thanks to the LORD for His goodness [chesed], and for His wonderful works to the children of men!   (verses 8, 15, 21, 31)

Then, in the last verse of Psalm 107, we find the word *chesed* again:

Whoever is wise will observe these things, and they will understand the lovingkindness [chesed] of the LORD.   (verse 43)

So, we see that God's mercy and lovingkindness are another aspect of His eternal nature.

6. Grace

God is also a God of grace. The writer of Hebrews said,

Let us therefore come boldly to the throne of grace, that we may obtain mercy and find grace to help in time of need.   (Hebrews 4:16)

This verse tells us that we need mercy, but then we need grace. Let's take a moment to absorb what the Bible says about grace. First and foremost, grace cannot be earned; it is a gift from God. If you could earn it, it wouldn't be grace. So, "religious" people have a real problem, because they believe they must earn everything. Consequently, they tend to turn down the grace of God. Paul said, "If it is of works, it is not of grace." Consequently, if it is of grace, it cannot be of works. (See Romans 4:4–5.)

You cannot earn mercy, and you cannot earn grace. When the writer of Hebrews said, *"Let us therefore come boldly to the throne of grace, that we may obtain mercy and find grace to help in time of need,"* it was a recognition that we need mercy for the past and grace for the future. Why? Because it is only by God's grace that we can become the kind of people, and live the kind of life, He requires of us.

7. Power

The last in this list of seven attributes of God is power. The whole Bible is full of passages that depict the power of God. Let's look at one example in Psalm 93:

The Lord reigns, He is clothed with majesty; the Lord is clothed, He has girded Himself with strength. Surely the world is established, so that it cannot be moved. Your throne is established from of old; You are from everlasting. The floods have lifted up, O Lord, the floods have lifted up their voice; the floods lift up their waves. The Lord on high is mightier than the noise of many waters, than the mighty waves of the sea.

(verses 1–4)

As we close this chapter, let us review the seven aspects of God's eternal nature:

1. Light
2. Love
3. Justice/Judgment

4. Anger/Wrath
5. Mercy/Lovingkindness (covenant-keeping faithfulness)
6. Grace
7. Power

Without a doubt, I believe that God's holiness encompasses all these attributes.

2

"Holy, Holy, Holy"

The whole Bible, from beginning to end, emphasizes the holiness of God. Yet when we read the translation of the Bible in English, it obscures a lot of facts about holiness. Certain words pertaining to holiness that are linked together in the original Greek language of the New Testament are not as clearly linked in English versions, which translate these words as *"holy," "saint,"* and *"sanctification."* If you were able to read the New Testament in Greek, the direct connection between these words would immediately be obvious by their root words. For this reason, I want to take a few moments to explain how these words are linked.

The basic Greek word normally translated as "holy" is *hagios*. In the King James Version, wherever you read the word *saints*, it is simply the plural of the adjective *holy*. So, *saints* means "holy ones." (I'm sure many sincere believers have never realized the true meaning of the word *saint*.)

Then, we have the English word *sanctify*. You don't have to be a teacher of English to realize that almost any word in English that ends in "i-f-y" means "to make something into whatever goes before the 'i-f-y.'" For instance, the verb *purify* means "to make pure." *Clarify* means "to make clear." *Rectify* means "to make right." By the same token, *sanctify* means "to make *sanct*." That doesn't make much sense until you realize that *sanct* is actually the same word as *saint*.

In German, as well as in all the Scandinavian languages, St. John, St. Luke, and the other "saints" are called Sankt Johann,

Sankt Lucas, and so on; therefore, the meaning is clearer. *Sanctify* means "to make *sanct*," or "to make saint." *Saint* means "holy," so, *sanctify* means "to make holy." It is very simple. The noun *sanctification*, therefore, stands for the process of "making holy."

Many believers are intimidated by a word like *sanctification*. It sounds so theological, difficult, and unpleasant that they want to avoid it. But the word *holy* has a beauty to it that attracts me. It is this beauty that I want to convey to you in this book.

For our future reference, let's remember that *saints* are "holy ones." *To sanctify* is "to make saint (saintly or holy)." And *sanctification* is simply "making holy." We will use these terms interchangeably from now on. In other words, when I use the word *sanctify*, I'm trusting that you will understand that it means "to make holy."

"High and Lifted Up"

In the next two chapters, we will look at some of the key passages in Scripture that speak about the holiness of God. We will begin with the depiction of God's holiness found in Isaiah 6. That passage describes a vision that was granted to the prophet Isaiah of the Lord on His throne in His glory. As I understand the book of Isaiah, the prophet was already a godly man, far above the level of the people of his day, before he received this wonderful vision. Even so, the vision had a tremendous impact upon him, as you will see. Let's begin with the first two verses:

> *In the year that King Uzziah died, I saw the Lord sitting on a throne, high and lifted up, and the train of His robe filled the temple. Above it stood seraphim; each one had six wings: with two he covered his face, with two he covered his feet, and with two he flew.*
> (Isaiah 6:1–2)

Let's consider for a moment the significance of the seraphim, these creatures whom Isaiah saw. We will note shortly that they are also revealed in a parallel passage in the fourth chapter of the book of Revelation. *Seraph* (the singular form of seraphim) in Hebrew means "that which burns." They are the burning ones.

The seraphim have six wings: four for worship, two for service. Please notice that the emphasis in this verse is on worship first and service second. With two wings, they covered their faces in worship and reverence. With two other wings, they covered their feet in worship and reverence. They used the remaining two wings to fly in service. This is the proper order and the right proportion. Worship comes before service. In many churches today, there is little or no appreciation of worship, but a great deal of activity with very little effective service.

The Threefold *"Holy"*

Let's continue on in Isaiah 6:

And one cried to another and said: "Holy, holy, holy is the LORD of hosts; the whole earth is full of His glory!" And the posts ["foundations" NASB] of the door were shaken by the voice of him who cried out, and the house was filled with smoke. (verses 3–4)

We see from this passage that all heaven is continually reminded of the holiness of God. Throughout eternity, this reminder of His holiness is given forth. The impact of the quality of holiness in almighty God is such that even the heavenly temple vibrates and trembles.

> **All heaven is continually reminded of the holiness of God.**

As Isaiah was caught up into heaven, he had this vision of worship in God's presence, in which he saw these seraphim—these burning, fiery creatures. As he listened, he heard them as *"one cried to another and said: 'Holy, holy, holy is the LORD of hosts.'"*

Isaiah 6:3 is one of only two passages in the Bible in which the adjective *"holy"* is applied to God three times. This same idea is carried over into the book of Revelation, which records how John was caught up likewise into heaven. He also heard the cries of the seraphim. They are not called *seraphim* in the Revelation passage, but they are the same beings. In Revelation, they are called *"living creatures"*:

> The four living creatures, each having six wings, were full of eyes around and within. And they do not rest day or night, saying: "Holy, holy, holy, Lord God Almighty, who was and is and is to come!" Whenever the living creatures give glory and honor and thanks to Him who sits on the throne, who lives forever and ever, the twenty-four elders fall down before Him who sits on the throne and worship Him who lives forever and ever, and cast their crowns before the throne, saying: "You are worthy, O Lord, to receive glory and honor and power."   (Revelation 4:8–11)

Again, *"holy"* is the only word that is used three times to describe God, both in the Old Testament and in the New Testament. In the Old Testament, the seraphim cry, *"Holy, holy, holy is the LORD of hosts"* (Isaiah 6:3). In the New Testament, the living creatures cry, *"Holy, holy, holy, Lord God Almighty"* (Revelation 4:8).

I believe there is a significance to the threefold repetition that is related to the tri-unity, or trinity, of God. It signifies that holy is the Father, holy is the Son, and holy is the Spirit. No one else is holy; holiness is uniquely descriptive of God. Therefore, as we saw earlier, we can understand or become partakers of holiness only insofar as we relate to God Himself. Holiness sums up His total being. When we see that the Bible uses the word *"holy"* three times to describe God, we realize that *holy* is the word that truly describes Him. As far as we know, the word is never applied apart from some reference to Him. Moving forward, we will see that holiness is not optional.

As the Scriptures tell us, *"Without* [holiness] *no one will see the Lord"* (Hebrews 12:14).

"A Man of Unclean Lips"

Let us now look at Isaiah's reaction to the holiness of the Lord:

> *Woe is me, for I am undone! Because I am a man of unclean lips, and I dwell in the midst of a people of unclean lips; for my eyes have seen the King, the LORD of hosts.* (Isaiah 6:5)

As I pointed out, by human standards Isaiah was a very godly man. However, this revelation of the holiness of God caused him to see himself in an entirely new light. He realized how far he was below the standard of God's holiness and heaven's holiness.

Please notice that when Isaiah became aware of his deficiency, there was one particular part of himself about which he was most acutely conscious, and in which he fell short. What was that? His *"lips."* James 3:2 says, *"If anyone does not stumble in word, he is a perfect man, able also to bridle the whole body."* Isaiah was brought face-to-face with the fact that he needed much more holiness than he had received to that point.

> **When we acknowledge our need, God is then ready with His provision.**

This is how God normally deals with you and me. He brings us to a sense of our need, and then He reveals His provision for the need. As we go on in this study, we will see that this process is true in relation to our need for holiness. When we acknowledge our need, God is then ready with His provision. As soon as Isaiah acknowledged his need, God's provision came to him:

Then one of the seraphim flew to me, having in his hand a live coal which he had taken with the tongs from the altar. And he touched my mouth with it, and said: "Behold, this has touched your lips; your iniquity is taken away, and your sin purged." (Isaiah 6:6–7)

The forgiveness of Isaiah's sin didn't come about by his own works. It wasn't a result of his own effort. Rather, it was due to the direct intervention of God. That coal from the altar is a symbol of the Holy Spirit. It is by the presence and power of the Holy Spirit that man is made holy.

The Call to Service

It was only after Isaiah had admitted his need and received God's provision to meet it that he heard the call to service. We see in Isaiah 6:8 how the prophet responded to the Lord's call:

Also I heard the voice of the Lord, saying: "Whom shall I send, and who will go for Us?" Then I said, "Here am I! Send me."

Basically (and I believe this is a reality that most Christians don't recognize), God does not use volunteers. We will see the truth of this statement in succeeding chapters. In our desire to serve the Lord, we first have to come to the place where we realize that we are ineffective and helpless. As long as you think you can do the job and that God is rather lucky to have you working for Him, there really isn't much that you can do of any permanent value for Him. However, when you come to the place where you realize that you are totally unfit, unable, and unworthy, then God will reach out His hand and touch your life.

My Call to Service

This passage dealing with Isaiah's confession of unclean lips and his response to God's call upon him is very meaningful to me because a similar experience took place in my life. The first time I went to a Pentecostal church service, accompanied by a fellow soldier in the British Army, it was somewhat of a shock to me. I came from a strong background in philosophy and had never been in such a service before. I had just one burning question: Does this preacher really know what he's talking about?

The preacher that evening took his text from the passage in Isaiah 6 that we have been examining. When he got to verse 5—*"I am a man of unclean lips, and I dwell in the midst of a people of unclean lips"*—something said to me, "No one ever described you more accurately than that!" From my experience in the British Army, I do not think there could have been any other group of men, anywhere, that better fit the designation of *"a people of unclean lips."*

After quoting that Scripture, he had my attention. I didn't know what he was talking about, but I realized that *he* did. And that was the door that opened to bring me to salvation.

The preacher had previously been a taxi driver—a different type of person from those I had listened to at Cambridge University. Although he had started with this text, he did not stick with it. He was one of those preachers who move from the Old Testament to the New and back again. Actually, I found him hard to follow.

At one point, he was talking about David the shepherd boy and his relationship with King Saul, and he conducted an imaginary dialogue between the two. He very rightly emphasized the fact that King Saul was head and shoulders taller than the rest of the people by jumping up on a little bench. When he was speaking as King Saul, he looked down at where he had been when he was speaking as David. I was following this presentation with some interest, but, in the midst of an impassioned speech as King Saul, the bench collapsed, and he fell to the floor with a loud thud. (Frankly, if you had been planning to prepare a presentation suitable for a professor from

Cambridge, you would have left that part out.) But, in spite of everything that happened—not *because* of everything, but *in spite of it*—I realized that he did know what he was talking about. Furthermore, I knew that *I* didn't.

When the preacher got to the end of this strange performance, he asked for every head to be bowed and every eye to be closed. I had never been in a setting where people bowed their heads like that and where, if a person wanted this experience, he would put his hand up. There was no background music—nothing. Just complete silence.

So, I sat there in what seemed to be a very long silence, and there were two inaudible voices speaking, one in each ear. One said, *If you put your hand up in front of these old ladies as a soldier in uniform, you're going to look very silly.* The other voice said, *If this is something good, why shouldn't you have it?*

Honestly, I was paralyzed. I could not respond. And then, a miracle took place. A real miracle. I saw my own right arm go up in the air, and I knew I had not raised it. At that point, I was really frightened. I thought, *What have I gotten myself into?*

Well, that was all that the people at the service were waiting for. The moment my arm went up, everything started moving again. I didn't receive any counseling from the pastor, but a very kind elderly couple who kept a boardinghouse near the church invited my fellow soldier and me home for supper. For soldiers in the army, that was a very tempting invitation.

As we walked back together with them, this little lady of about sixty told me about her experiences. She described how her husband had been exempted from military service in World War I because he'd had tuberculosis. I knew that if it had gained him an exemption, it must have been a valid medical diagnosis. Then, she said to me, "I prayed every day for ten years for God to heal my husband." I thought to myself, *This is a dimension I have never even thought of—to pray every day for ten years for something.* She continued, "One particular day, I was in the parlor praying. My husband was sitting up in bed in the bedroom spitting up blood. I heard a voice say, 'Claim it.' And I answered, 'Lord, I claim it now.'" At that very moment, her husband was completely healed. *Well*, I said to myself, *maybe this is what I've been looking for.*

The Need for Humility

That was my introduction to the Pentecostal movement, and that was how God used this passage from Isaiah 6 as my calling into service for Him, as unprepared for and unfamiliar with that entire realm as I was.

> **Isaiah had to be humble in the presence of God's holiness before he was qualified for the task.**

Every man whose life I have studied in the Scriptures who was called by God to a special job felt he was unfit to do that job. If you ever meet a person who says he is called by God and is fully able to do the job, you can be almost sure he was not called by God.

So, Isaiah had to be humble, he had to be brought low in the presence of God's holiness, before he was qualified for the task to which the Lord wanted to call him. The same will be true for you.

3

HOLINESS THROUGHOUT SCRIPTURE

In this chapter, we will look more closely at the Scripture in Revelation 4 that lines up with the passage in Isaiah 6, along with some other passages on holiness. I love the book of Revelation. At one time, I said to my wife Ruth, "I just don't understand the book of Revelation. I don't get much out of it. Let's read it right through." So, we did.

Afterward, I said, "I still didn't get much out of it. Let's read it through again." And we did.

The third time, something opened up to me. From that point on, if I had to choose what passage I would like to read, most often, I would choose either Revelation 4 or 5, because that section of Scripture describes a scene of worship in heaven. Again, within those chapters, as in the Isaiah 6 passage, the word *"holy"* is applied three times to the Lord.

Lifted to the Throne Level

Revelation 4 is a glorious chapter, the key word and central theme of which is *"throne."* Let's examine this whole chapter, counting how many times the word *"throne"* is mentioned in it.

After these things I looked, and behold, a door standing open in heaven. And the first voice which I heard was like a trumpet speaking with me, saying, "Come up here, and I will show you things which must take place after this." Immediately I was in the Spirit; and behold, a throne set in heaven [the first thing he saw was the throne], *and One sat on the throne.*

(Revelation 4:1–2)

So far, we have two mentions of the word *"throne."*

And He who sat there was like a jasper and a sardius stone in appearance; and there was a rainbow around the throne, in appearance like an emerald. Around the throne were twenty-four thrones, and on the thrones I saw twenty-four elders sitting, clothed in white robes; and they had crowns of gold on their heads. And from the throne proceeded lightnings, thunderings, and voices. Seven lamps of fire were burning before the throne, which are the seven Spirits of God. Before the throne there was a sea of glass, like crystal. And in the midst of the throne, and around the throne, were four living creatures full of eyes in front and in back. [These correspond to the seraphim Isaiah saw.] *The first living creature was like a lion, the second living creature like a calf, the third living creature had a face like a man, and the fourth living creature was like a flying eagle. The four living creatures, each having six wings, were full of eyes around and within. And they do not rest day or night, saying: "Holy, holy, holy, Lord God Almighty, who was and is and is to come!" Whenever the living creatures give glory and honor and thanks to Him who sits on the throne, who lives forever and ever, the twenty-four elders fall down before Him who sits on the throne and worship Him who lives forever and ever, and cast their crowns before the throne, saying: "You are worthy, O Lord, to receive glory and honor and power; for You created all things, and by Your will they exist and were created."* (verses 3–11)

Did you count the number of "thrones"? In a single chapter of only eleven verses, the words *"throne"* or *"thrones"* occur fourteen times. The Scriptures reveal that there are four main orders of the invisible, created world, and Paul listed them in Colossians 1:16 as follows: *"thrones,"* *"dominions,"* *"principalities,"* and *"powers."* The highest level of the created order of the universe is the throne level.

In this fourth chapter of Revelation, the apostle John is lifted up to the throne level. This scene, therefore, takes place at the highest level of creation, and, on that level, there is one continual theme: *"Holy, holy, holy."* As I indicated earlier, this threefold declaration speaks of the triune God: Father, Son, and Spirit. Holy is the Father, holy is the Son, and holy is the Spirit. Again, all heaven is constantly reminded

> *"Holy, holy, holy"* **speaks of the triune God: Father, Son, and Spirit.**

of this fact. Surely, it would be appropriate if those of us on earth were a little more mindful of the same fact—in particular, those of us who are the members of Christ's body, the church.

Let's consider a few additional salient points from this passage. It is significant that the first object John saw when he was caught up in the Spirit was a throne. Then, when his eyes had adjusted to the throne, he could see the Person who was seated on the throne. John was seeing the throne room of God, the place from which the universe is governed.

Next, John saw the living creatures—fiery beings—and heard them crying, *"Holy, holy, holy, Lord God Almighty."* There is something about holiness that is fiery, and that interests me a great deal. Just prior to mentioning the fiery creatures, this passage talks of the *"seven lamps of fire"* (Revelation 4:5), which is another visible presentation of the Holy Spirit. Hebrews 12:29 says, *"For our God is a consuming fire."* It does not say that God is *like* a consuming fire; He *is* a consuming fire. The *"fire"* in this Revelation passage is not God the Father, nor is it God the Son. It is God the Holy Spirit. He is a consuming fire.

When the fire fell on the sacrifice of Elijah on Mount Carmel, all the people fell flat on their faces, shouting, *"The Lord, He is God!"* (1 Kings 18:39). They fell on their faces because they were present before God Himself, not a mere spiritual manifestation. They were present before the third person of the Godhead, the One who is a living flame of fire.

"Glorious in Holiness"

In the last chapter, we discussed the theme of holiness in Isaiah 6:3. Let us now look at some additional Scriptures in the Old Testament that speak about the holiness of God. We will briefly go through them in order. The first is Exodus 15:11:

> *Who is like You, O Lord, among the gods? Who is like You, glorious in holiness, fearful* ["*awesome*" NASB, NIV] *in praises, doing wonders?*

God is glorious in His holiness. And, when we see His holiness, He becomes fearful or awesome, inspiring us to praise Him. When we praise Him, He then does wonders. There is a beautiful revelation there. When you appreciate the holiness of God, you praise Him as He should be praised. When you praise Him as He should be praised, the wonders begin to flow. That is the divine order.

"He Is a Holy God"

We move next to the last chapter of the book of Joshua, in which Joshua challenged God's people Israel after they had come into their inheritance, the Promised Land. The challenge he put before them was essentially this: "Who are you going to serve, now that you're in your land?" Joshua gave them this choice: "*'Choose for yourselves this day whom you will serve.'* You can serve the gods that your fathers served on the other side of the river Euphrates in Mesopotamia. Or, you can serve the gods of the Amorites, whose lands you now dwell in. Or, you can serve the true and living God, the Lord." (See Joshua 24:15.) And the people responded that they would serve the Lord:

> *So the people answered and said: "Far be it from us that we should forsake the LORD to serve other gods."*
>
> (verse 16)

Then, the people gave a recitation of God's greatness, His victories, and His blessings. In response, Joshua came back with a rather surprising reply:

> *You cannot serve the LORD, for He is a holy God. He is a jealous God; He will not forgive your transgressions nor your sins.* (verse 19)

Earlier, I said that God is not looking for volunteers. This is what I meant by that statement. So many in the contemporary church say, "I think I want to serve the Lord. I wonder if God has a job for me." As long as you approach almighty God with that attitude, you are not going to make contact with Him. Again, I believe that most Christians today have the impression that God was rather lucky to get their services when they were saved. God doesn't see it that way.

> **Most Christians have the impression that God was rather lucky to get their services when they were saved.**

For a good many years, I had that attitude, because I had been somewhat accomplished in the professional and academic worlds. Years later, I began to see that it was a totally different story. God had accepted tremendous responsibilities when He accepted me. You cannot just walk up to the Lord and say, "God, I think I'm going to serve You." God says, "You can't do it. You're not qualified. You're not equipped. You'll fail, and then you'll be worse off than you were before."

We need to bear this thought in mind: before we offer service to God, we had better remember the kind of God we are serving. He is a holy God. A glorious God. A fearful God.

We cannot fool around in His service. It is not a matter of playing little religious games. It is not a matter of attending church now and then, whenever it suits us. Unless it is a total commitment, it has very little value.

"No One Is Holy like the Lord"

The theme of God's holiness is brought up again in 1 Samuel, where we see it in the song of Hannah after God had granted her the baby she had been longing for. Allow me to make just a brief observation regarding the passage in 1 Samuel 1 when Hannah was fretting. I would say that a fretting woman is often a barren woman. But when Hannah got the victory in faith and ceased fretting, she conceived and became a mother. In chapter 2, she had a note of victory in her song of praise.

> *And Hannah prayed and said: "My heart rejoices in the LORD; my horn is exalted in the LORD. I smile at my enemies, because I rejoice in Your salvation. No one is holy like the LORD, for there is none besides You, nor is there any rock like our God."* (1 Samuel 2:1–2)

In moments of real spiritual victory and discernment, we always come to see that God is unique. He is holy, and there is none other like Him in the whole universe.

Enthroned upon the Praises of His People

Then, in the Psalms, we have another beautiful revelation of the holiness of God and our proper reaction to it. The psalmist said, *"You are holy, enthroned in [*"upon"* NASB] the praises of Israel"* (Psalm 22:3). The King James Version translates the verse as, *"Thou art holy, O thou that inhabitest the praises of Israel,"* but I prefer *"enthroned in"* to *"inhabitest."* I was once talking about this verse with a Swedish friend who is a singer. I had been preaching on the topic of praise and about the translation of Psalm 22:3 in a Swedish version of the Bible, which we would render in English as, "Thou who art enthroned upon the praises of Israel." It had been a real revelation to me. Then, my Swedish friend said this to me: "A king is a king, whether he has a throne or not. The Lord is a King, whether He has a throne or not. But when we praise Him, we offer Him His throne to sit upon. And then, in His kingly presence, He is among us."

God sits enthroned upon the praises of His people. But we must recognize that praise is the outcome of the recognition of His holiness. *"You are holy, enthroned in the praises of Israel."*

The High and Lofty One Who Dwells with the Humble

Next, we come to another beautiful verse in Isaiah:

For thus says the High and Lofty One who inhabits eternity, whose name is Holy: "I dwell in the high and holy place, with him who has a contrite and humble spirit, to revive the spirit of the humble, and to revive the heart of the contrite ones." (Isaiah 57:15)

I am so gripped by the beauty of this verse that I want to make sure we touch on its salient features. The Holy One says, *"I dwell in the high and holy place, with him who has a contrite and humble spirit."* My initial comment is that God's holiness provokes man's humility. When we really see the holiness of God, there is only one condition that will result in us, and that is humility.

Notice that there are actually three words that run like a theme through the above verse, and each of these words occurs twice. In addition, each begins with the letter *h*: the *High* and Lofty One, whose name is *Holy*, dwells in the *high* and *holy* place with the *humble*, to revive the spirit of the one who is *humble*. The theme of this verse is "high, holy, and humble."

If you want God to dwell with you, offer Him a humble heart. The One who inhabits eternity and whose throne is above the heavens will dwell with the one *"who has a contrite and humble spirit."* I don't believe that anybody who is living in the revelation of the holiness of God can be proud, because pride is really a denial of God's holiness.

I hope this brief examination of the above Scriptures has helped you to better understand the nature of God's holiness. We will move on now to see how God expects His people to walk in holiness.

4

GOD REQUIRES HOLINESS

Not only is God holy, but He also requires holiness in His people. In exploring this topic, we will examine a number of Scriptures from Leviticus, because the theme of the book of Leviticus is holiness—the word *"holy"* occurs there more than ninety times.

> *For I am the LORD your God. You shall therefore conse-crate yourselves [consecrate means "to "sanctify" or "to make holy"], and you shall be holy; for I am holy. Neither shall you defile yourselves with any creeping thing that creeps on the earth. For I am the LORD who brings you up out of the land of Egypt, to be your God. You shall therefore be holy, for I am holy.*
> (Leviticus 11:44–45)

> *Speak to all the congregation of the children of Israel, and say to them: "You shall be holy, for I the LORD your God am holy."*
> (Leviticus 19:2)

> *Consecrate [sanctify] yourselves therefore, and be holy, for I am the LORD your God.*
> (Leviticus 20:7)

> *And you shall be holy to Me, for I the LORD am holy, and have separated you from the peoples, that you should be Mine.*
> (verse 26)

"Be Holy, for I Am Holy"

By clear implication of the Scriptures, the requirement for being God's people is to be holy as He is holy. This quality is what distinguishes and separates us from all other people on the earth.

Let us turn briefly to Leviticus 10:10:

That you may distinguish between holy and unholy, and between unclean and clean.

One of the main themes of the book of Leviticus is how to distinguish between what is holy and what is unholy, between what is clean and what is unclean. In fact, one of the main responsibilities of the priesthood under the law of Moses was to teach God's people the difference between holy and unholy. The failure of the priesthood to do so was one of the main causes of spiritual and national disaster in Israel.

> **One of the great responsibilities of ministers is to teach what is holy and what is unholy.**

This same principle applies to Christian ministry. One of the great responsibilities of the ministers of God's people is to teach the true nature of holiness, including how to distinguish between what is holy and what is unholy. Where this teaching is not given, or is not received, spiritual disaster will always follow.

Missing Pieces in Understanding Holiness

One of the greatest missing pieces in the church's understanding of holiness is the practice of fasting. It has dropped almost entirely out of the picture, and the church cannot have a complete conception of the holiness of God without it. Connected to this missing piece is the loss of intercession leading up to fasting. To me, a passage in Isaiah 59 is a picture of our contemporary society. It begins,

> *Justice is turned back, and righteousness stands afar off; for truth is fallen in the street, and equity cannot enter.* (verse 14)

(When I survey the current political scene, I just say to myself, *Truth has fallen in the street.*)

The passage continues,

> *So truth fails, and he who departs from evil makes himself a prey.* (verse 15)

I believe we are getting very near that stage. You do not have to be actively or aggressively righteous to be persecuted in society today. You simply have to refrain from evil, and people will notice you and pick on you. Here was the Lord's reaction to the situation in which truth failed and he who departed from evil made himself a prey:

> *Then the LORD saw it, and it displeased Him that there was no justice. He saw that there was no man, and wondered that there was no intercessor.* (verses 15–16)

That last phrase could accurately describe God's attitude toward many sections of the church today. He wonders at the fact that there are no intercessors.

Plastering with Untempered Mortar

We see a similar truth in Ezekiel 22, which highlights God's emphasis on intercession. In the passage below, there are four groups that are charged with delinquency, and they all begin with the letter *p*. This is the order of those groups: the prophets, the priests, the princes, and the people. Please notice that God does not begin with the princes, the secular rulers. He begins with those who profess faith in Him—the prophets and the priests. If you can trace the trouble to its cause, that is where it begins. Secular rulers may be evil, but they are never the primary source of evil. It is those who claim to represent God with no true evidence of doing so who are the primary source of the problem.

We begin with Ezekiel 22:24, where the Lord was speaking to the prophet Ezekiel:

> *Son of man, say to her* [Israel]: *"You are a land that is not cleansed or rained on in the day of indignation."*

In the late 1950s, I was teaching in Kenya, and one of my students read this verse and commented, "The only thing that can cleanse a land is the rain of the Holy Spirit." That observation has never departed from me. A land that has not received the rain of the Holy Spirit is not cleansed. Then, the Lord continued,

> *The conspiracy of her prophets in her midst is like a roaring lion....Her priests have violated My law and profaned My holy things; they have not distinguished between the holy and unholy....Her princes in her midst are like wolves tearing the prey....Her prophets plastered* [the people] *with untempered mortar....The people of the land have used oppressions, committed robbery, and mistreated the poor and needy.*
>
> (verses 25–29)

I feel that, basically, the church is plastering believers with untempered mortar, which will all be washed away when the rain and the floods come. We are not confronting the basic issues of sin and righteousness and responsibility.

Again, in Ezekiel 22:29, we read, *"The people of the land have used oppressions."* Please note that the people are the last to be blamed. We can accuse the drug addicts and the "sinners," but they are at the end of the story. The trouble begins with the prophets and then the priests—the clergy.

Standing in the Gap

Then, we come to the climax of Ezekiel 22:

So I sought for a man among them who would make a wall, and stand in the gap before Me on behalf of the land, that I should not destroy it; but I found no one.

(verse 30)

What a tragic statement: *"But I found no one"*—not one person. Notice that the person God sought was expected to do two things. First, he was to build up a wall. Generally, in our contemporary culture, all the walls of natural separation have been broken down—particularly, in my opinion, the separation between male and female, which is basic. It was the original separation instituted at creation, and I have lived long enough to see this separation broken down, sometimes through acts of law, before my eyes.

God was looking for this person to not only rebuild the walls of separation but also restore the boundaries. Finally, he was to stand in the gap before Him—to stand between the people and the Lord as an intercessor. *Intercessor* means "one who comes in between."

For example, Abraham was an intercessor on behalf of the people of the city of Sodom. When the Lord and two angels visited Abraham's home, Abraham stood between the Lord and Sodom and bargained with the Lord, reducing the required number of righteous men from fifty to ten. The Lord eventually said, in effect, "If I find ten righteous, I'll spare the city for their sake." Unfortunately, He did not find even ten, but Abraham standing between the Lord and the objects of His wrath is a perfect picture of the intercessor—the one who stands in between. (See Genesis 18.)

Another description of an intercessor is a person who comes from among his own people, stands before God, and says, "If You strike them, Lord, You're going to have to strike me first." That is the intercessor.

As a nation, we have departed so far from God, His standards, and all that we know to be righteous that, unless we can truly humble ourselves before Him and call upon His mercy, there is no hope. Hope is not in the politician. It is not even in the church leaders. Hope is in a humble minority who will afflict their souls with fasting and intercession. But these, again, are missing elements of holiness and righteous actions that ought to be found in the church.

Self-denial was a major theme of the writings of nineteenth-century Christian leaders. Today, I never hear it taught. We are in a very different frame of mind from the people Paul urged to *"pursue...holiness"* (Hebrews 12:14). To pursue something is to aim for it and to go for it with all your might. You may have to run fast, or you may have to surmount obstacles, but you are following hard after this pursuit.

Your impressions may be different from mine, but, as I wrote in the introduction, I honestly cannot think of any group of people I have ministered to and been among who were truly pursuing holiness. In my book *They Shall Expel Demons*, I included an analogy of the contemporary church's attitude toward holiness. I put it in terms of a tour package. At one time in our lives, my wife Ruth and I organized tours, so we were very familiar with the process. People can purchase the basic tour package, and then, if they want to do something additional, it becomes an add-on, or an option, for which they can pay a little extra. For example, suppose a group is quoted a certain price for a trip to the Holy Land, but, for two hundred dollars extra, they can add a boat trip up the Nile River. The excursion up the Nile is an option that they don't have to take.

I believe a lot of Christians in the contemporary church regard salvation as the trip to the Holy Land and holiness as the optional excursion up the Nile. Holiness is treated as an "add-on," but nobody bothers to pay for it. I am not attacking anyone; I am just being objective, as far as my own impressions are concerned. Holiness is not an "add-on" in God's provision. It is an essential part of His salvation, and He expects it of His people. In fact, holiness is to be our distinguishing mark, as we will see in the next chapter.

> **Holiness is not an "add-on." It is an essential part of salvation.**

5

THE DISTINCTIVE FEATURE OF GOD'S PEOPLE

In this chapter, we will look at corresponding Scriptures from the Old and New Testaments which support this premise: the distinguishing mark of God's people is to be their holiness.

A Special Treasure

First, in Exodus 19, God says to His people,

Now therefore, if ye will obey my voice indeed, and keep my covenant, then ye shall be a peculiar ["special" NKJV] treasure unto me above all people: for all the earth is mine: and ye shall be unto me a kingdom of priests, and an holy nation. (verses 5–6 KJV)

To be God's people, we have to be different—different in terms of holiness, separated out from all other peoples. The word *peculiar*, used in the above Scripture, has undergone a change in meaning somewhat from the days of the King James Version, when it meant "distinct, unlike anything else, separate."

In Deuteronomy 14, we find almost the same wording as in the Exodus passage. The book of Deuteronomy is essentially an analysis of the conditions for entering into your God-given inheritance and staying in it. And, like Leviticus, Deuteronomy puts great emphasis on holiness:

> *For you are a holy people to the LORD your God, and the LORD has chosen you to be a ["peculiar" KJV] people for Himself, a special treasure above all the peoples who are on the face of the earth.* (Deuteronomy 14:2)

We see in this passage that the unique distinctive feature of God's people is their holiness. It is this trait that distinguishes them from all other peoples. And it is this trait that lifts them up. We cannot live on the plane that God desires us to live on unless we live and walk in holiness. This truth is stated very clearly in Deuteronomy 26:18–19. Let's begin with the first part of verse 18:

> *Also today the LORD has proclaimed ["avouched" KJV] you to be His special ["peculiar" KJV] people....*

The word *"proclaimed"* means "publicly acknowledged." God publicly acknowledges His people as being distinct from all other people.

> *...just as He promised you, that you should keep all His commandments, and that He will set you high above all nations which He has made, in praise, in name, and in honor, and that you may be a holy people to the LORD your God, just as He has spoken.* (verses 18–19)

If we want to be *"high above,"* we have to be holy. These two qualities cannot be separated. God wants His people to live on a high plane, not to be under the dominion of situations and circumstances and the attacks of the enemy. He wants us to be a victorious, reigning people. But the condition is holiness.

Conditions of Holiness in the Old Testament Carried Over into the New

We will now take note of how these requirements of the Old Testament are carried over word for word into the New Testament. In 1 Peter, the apostle Peter actually quoted the Old Testament passages that we have already examined as he wrote to his Christian audience.

> ...but as He who called you is holy, you also be holy in all your conduct, because it is written, "Be holy, for I am holy." (1 Peter 1:15–16)

In this passage, Peter quoted from Leviticus, saying, in essence, "Remember, the same truth applies to you Christians that applied to Israel under the Law." Then, we see in 1 Peter 2:9:

> But you are a chosen generation, a royal priesthood, a holy nation, His own special ["peculiar" KJV] people....

All the phrases in the above verse were taken from the several passages of the Old Testament we have looked at. They are just compiled in this one verse to describe Christian believers. The verse tells us why we are called to be holy:

> But you are a chosen generation, a royal priesthood, a holy nation, His own special ["peculiar" KJV] people, that you may proclaim ["show forth" KJV] the praises of Him who called you out of darkness into His marvelous light. (verse 9)

The revelation of God's holiness will always cause us to show forth His praises. A person who does not praise God has very little conception of His holiness. Where God's holiness is revealed, it stirs us up to praise. We *"proclaim"* His praises, meaning that we demonstrate His nature and qualities to those around us.

Moving to the book of Revelation, chapter 1, we read,

To Him who loved us and washed us from our sins in His own blood, and has made us kings and priests to His God and Father.... (verses 5–6)

In the Old Testament, the equivalent phrase to *"kings and priests"* is *"a kingdom of priests"* (Exodus 19:6). Actually, that is a more literal translation of what the New Testament says: a kingdom of priests. The same thought is found in Revelation 5:

And they sang a new song, saying: "You are worthy to take the scroll, and to open its seals; for You were slain, and have redeemed us to God by Your blood out of every tribe and tongue and people and nation, and have made us kings and priests to our God; and we shall reign on the earth." (Revelation 5:9–10)

Through God's provision, every believer is a king and a priest. What is the function of a king? It is to rule. What is the function of a priest? It is twofold: to offer sacrifices and to intercede. As believers in Christ, we have already been made kings and priests to rule, to offer sacrifices, and to intercede. This is not something that is expected of us in the future. It has already occurred, as we take our places in Christ and in His holiness.

Please notice how all these Old Testament and New Testament verses correspond to one another: *"You shall therefore be holy, for I am holy"* (Leviticus 11:45) is quoted in 1 Peter 1:16: *"Be holy, for I am holy."* *"A kingdom of priests and a holy nation"* (Exodus 19:6) is carried over into Revelation 1:6 and 5:10: *"kings and priests."* It is the same language. Again, both Deuteronomy 28:18–19 and 1 Peter 2:9 contain the same ideas: "A chosen generation," "a holy nation," and "a special (peculiar) people."

Clearly, the distinction of God's people is their holiness. It is the indication above all others that we belong to Him.

6

THE CLEANSING WE NEED

We turn our focus now to other writings in the New Testament that emphasize holiness. We will start with the writings of the apostle Paul, beginning in 2 Corinthians 7:

> *Therefore, having these promises, beloved, let us cleanse ourselves from all filthiness of the flesh and spirit, perfecting holiness in the fear of God.*
>
> (verse 1)

In this verse, Paul laid out the challenge to believers in Christ: we have to cleanse ourselves. Please notice that the responsibility is put clearly upon us. It is what we have to do. We have to perfect, or complete, holiness *"in the fear of God."*

Also, observe that this passage directs us to cleanse ourselves from two different kinds of filthiness: *"filthiness of the flesh"* and *"filthiness of the...spirit."* Filthiness of the flesh refers to obvious carnal sins—fornication, drunkenness, blasphemy, and so on. But filthiness of the spirit is that forbidden interaction with Satan's kingdom: seeking after occult, supernatural, satanic powers in the form of such things as fortune-telling, divination, witchcraft, sorcery, and idolatry. The Bible signifies that such interaction is "spiritual adultery." (See, for example, 1 Corinthians 10:19–23.) In God's sight, it is far more serious than even physical adultery. The Scriptures say that, in view of God's promises, we are under an obligation to cleanse ourselves in both areas—the area of the flesh and the area of the spirit.

By so cleansing ourselves, we are *"perfecting holiness in the fear of God."*

Reasons for Cleansing

Let me point out that the first word of 2 Corinthians 7:1 is *"Therefore"*: *"Therefore, having these promises...."* You may be familiar with one of my favorite sayings, which is, "When you find a *therefore* in the Bible, you want to find out what it's 'there for.'" The word *therefore* in the above verse refers to the promises of God from the Old Testament that are quoted at the end of 2 Corinthians chapter 6. Specifically, the last two verses of that chapter read as follows:

> Therefore *"Come out from among them and be separate, says the Lord. Do not touch what is unclean, and I will receive you. I will be a Father to you, and you shall be My sons and daughters, says the LORD Almighty."*
>
> (verses 17–18)

The condition for God receiving us is that we come out and be separate and do not touch what is unclean.

Then, as we have seen, Paul went on to say,

> *Therefore, having these promises, beloved, let us cleanse ourselves..., perfecting holiness in the fear of God.* (2 Corinthians 7:1)

In other words, on the basis of God's promises and requirements, we are to perfect holiness in our lives as a demonstration of our reverence for God.

"Blameless in Holiness"

Let us look next at several important passages on holiness found in the first epistle to the Thessalonians. In many ways, the Thessalonians had been model converts to Christ. They had come to the Lord with great joy and excitement. Their lifestyles had been transformed. They were living witnesses. The Word of God sounded out from them to the regions round about. But we have to remember that they had formerly lived in abject paganism and heathenism, and there were many truths about God that they still did not know. If you did not realize this, you might be surprised at some of the things that Paul had to tell them.

One of the truths he had to emphasize was the principle of holiness, or sanctification. They had not yet come to understand much of this principle, and so you will see the theme of sanctification running throughout Paul's first letter to them. We will examine this theme in three successive passages, beginning with 1 Thessalonians 3. This was Paul's desire and prayer for these believers:

> And may the Lord make you increase and abound in love to one another and to all, just as we do to you, so that He may establish your hearts blameless in holiness before our God and Father at the coming of our Lord Jesus Christ with all His saints [holy ones].
>
> (verses 12–13)

The teaching of holiness is always linked with the expectation of Christ's return.

Paul was looking forward to one tremendous event, which is the coming of the Lord Jesus Christ. I believe that if you read the New Testament with an open mind, you will discover this vital truth: the teaching of holiness is always linked with the expectation of Christ's imminent return. The New Testament Christians lived in the hourly expectation that Jesus would be coming back. Consequently, this was their greatest motivation for pursuing and maintaining holiness in their lives.

I believe we cannot live in holiness as they lived unless we have the same expectation they had. The coming of the Lord is the hope written about in 1 John 3:2–3 that causes a believer to purify himself:

Beloved, now we are children of God; and it has not yet been revealed what we shall be, but we know that when He [Jesus] is revealed, we shall be like Him, for we shall see Him as He is. And everyone who has this hope in Him purifies himself, just as He is pure.

I was once talking to a sweet lady, the wife of a pastor from an old-line denomination, who had been baptized in the Holy Spirit. We were talking about this theme, and I began to speak about the fact that the coming of the Lord is very close at hand. In a very nice way, she began to try to cool me off, telling me that I was not to get too excited. "People also believed this in the year one thousand, and they believed it in the days of Wesley. There were many people throughout church history who believed it, and still the Lord hasn't come." I replied, "Nevertheless, I believe He's coming, and coming soon."

This lady and I did not have an argument, and I really think I pleased the Lord by replying the way I did. I went to bed that night at peace, and I received a little extra reward in the morning, when I woke with something inside me that said, "Jesus is coming soon." I don't mind telling you that I have never been quite as excited about the coming of the Lord as I was at that point.

From that point onward, my prayers to the Lord were ever stronger that I would never lose that inner conviction that Jesus is coming soon. Believe me, it is the real motivation for holy living. Paul said, in effect, "Remember, you're going to meet Jesus. Just imagine how you're going to have to be at that great hour." That is the motivation Paul described in 1 Thessalonians 3:13: *"So that He may establish your hearts blameless in holiness before our God and Father at the coming of our Lord Jesus Christ with all His saints [holy ones]."*

Again, the second coming of Jesus Christ is the great incentive to personal holiness. Please notice in the above verse where holiness begins. It begins in the *heart*. God's most valuable work always begins in the heart.

A Clean Vessel

In the next chapter of 1 Thessalonians, Paul progressed to talking about holiness in relation to our bodies:

> *For this is the will of God, your sanctification: that you should abstain from sexual immorality* ["fornication" KJV]; *that each of you should know how to possess his own vessel in sanctification and honor.*
> (1 Thessalonians 4:3–4)

As I mentioned earlier, it may be a little surprising to us that Paul had to tell Christians that they were not free to commit sexual immorality any longer. But these people came from a pagan background without the Ten Commandments and without any accepted standards of morality. Paul had to tell them that fornication is not permitted for a Christian. Some people today give it a fancier name and call it "premarital sex," but the same truth still applies.

Your body is a wonderful creation that was designed to be a temple of the Holy Spirit.

Verse 4 says that *"each of you should know how to possess his own vessel in sanctification and honor."* What is meant by *"his own vessel"*? Paul was speaking of the physical body. In effect he was saying, "As a Christian, you have to know how to keep the vessel of your physical body in holiness and honor. You must learn how to keep that body of yours pure, clean, healthy, and available to the Spirit of God."

Your body is honorable. It is a wonderful creation of God that was designed to be a temple of the Holy Spirit (see 1 Corinthians 3:16; 6:19), and it is your personal responsibility to keep that temple in the best possible condition, from every point of view. For example, I do not think any sincere believer can neglect the health of his own body, because the body is so closely tied in with God's purposes of holiness.

Paul gave similar instructions to the Romans: *"Do not present your members as instruments of unrighteousness to sin, but present...your members as instruments of righteousness to God"* (Romans 6:13). I do not agree with anybody who deliberately breaks down the condition of his physical body in any way. Holiness is not just a list of "don'ts," a fact I will emphasize throughout this book. However, anything that actually causes the condition of the physical body to deteriorate is unholy—no matter what it may be.

Sanctified Completely

The final verse we will examine is from the fifth chapter of 1 Thessalonians. In this chapter, Paul returned to the theme of holiness and summed it up in one of the most glorious phrases of all Scripture:

> *And the very God of peace sanctify you wholly....*
> (1 Thessalonians 5:23 KJV)

Wholly means "entirely" or "completely." This is doubtless the verse from which the phrase "entire sanctification," a concept emphasized in some denominations, is taken. Rightly understood, entire sanctification is a scriptural doctrine. But it is not to be confused with the extreme teaching of "sinless perfection," which is not what the Bible teaches. Paul prayed here that these people would be sanctified wholly, entirely, completely. Then, he was very specific as to what that meant:

> *And the very God of peace sanctify you wholly; and*
> *I pray God your whole spirit and soul and body be*

> *preserved blameless unto the coming of our Lord Jesus*
> *Christ. Faithful is he that calleth you, who also will do*
> *it.* (1 Thessalonians 5:23–24 KJV)

Please notice again that the motivation for personal holiness is the coming of our Lord Jesus Christ. In view of this event, Paul's mandate is to keep yourself—spirit, soul, and body—clean, pure, and ready. Sanctification applies to every area of life. When Jesus comes, He is coming for a complete personality. And that personality needs to be sanctified, holy, set apart for God.

7

A REVELATION OF GOD'S HOLINESS

The book of Job describes a revelation of God's sovereignty and holiness that we will unfold in this chapter. My wife Ruth and I frequently studied Job together, and it was always an enriching experience. One time, after we had just finished reading the book again, I remarked to her, "No one can explain God." I believe it is very important for us to understand that it is impossible to fully explain God. He is unfathomable, and He is totally sovereign.

My definition of sovereignty is this: God does what He wants, when He wants, the way He wants, and He asks no one's permission. In contrast to that, contemporary culture has the attitude, "Well, if God is going to do something, He needs my permission." Again, people who think in that way will experience a rude awakening.

God Is Sovereign in Our Lives

One of the most striking discoveries I made as I was meditating on Job's experiences was the amazing way in which God dealt with him. In a sense, God handed Job over to Satan and said, "You can go so far, Satan, but no further." Satan was in control of the negative situations in Job's life, but we need to recognize the fact that Satan could do these things only when God released him.

> **God's supreme objective was to bring Job to a face-to-face revelation of Him.**

Another amazing fact was that Job was the most righteous man in his generation. (See Job 1:8.) So, what was God's purpose in all that happened to him? My opinion is that God used every negative thing that Satan did to Job in order to bring Job to the place where he could have a face-to-face revelation of Him. That was the supreme objective.

Let's take a few moments to consider what God expended to bring this one man, Job, to an encounter with Himself.

The Man from Uz

> *There was a man in the land of Uz, whose name was Job; and that man was blameless and upright, and one who feared God and shunned evil....Then the* Lord *said to Satan, "Have you considered My servant Job, that there is none like him on the earth, a blameless and upright man, one who fears God and shuns evil?"* (Job 1:1, 8)

These verses contain some remarkable facts. First, Satan had access to the presence of the Lord. He does at times, and I have reconciled myself to that fact. But more amazing is the fact that the Lord pointed Job out to Satan. He said, "Have you ever met a man like this, Satan?"

Of course, Satan had a nasty retort, saying, in effect, "Well, look what he gets for it. You take care of him in every way. You provide for everything." So, the Lord said, "Fine. You can take it all away, but don't touch him."

Let's see what Job had when he started out and what he lost:

His possessions were seven thousand sheep, three thousand camels, five hundred yoke of oxen, five hundred female donkeys, and a very large household, so that this man was the greatest of all the people of the East. (Job 1:3)

All of those possessions went away through Satan's destructions—not only the animals, but almost all of the servants who looked after them. In verses 14–15, we read,

A messenger came to Job and said, "The oxen were plowing and the donkeys feeding beside them, when the Sabeans raided them and took them away; indeed they have killed the servants with the edge of the sword; and I alone have escaped to tell you!"

All five hundred yoke of oxen and five hundred female donkeys were taken, and all but one of the servants looking after them were killed. Then, we read in verse 16:

While he was still speaking, another also came and said, "The fire of God fell from heaven and burned up the sheep and the servants, and consumed them; and I alone have escaped to tell you!"

Seven thousand sheep perished. I want to mention here that the *"fire of God"* was at the command of Satan. It does not mean that God sent it; that is merely what the people called it.

Again, only one servant survived. In verse 17, we read,

While he was still speaking, another also came and said, "The Chaldeans formed three bands, raided the camels and took them away, yes, and killed the servants with the edge of the sword; and I alone have escaped to tell you!"

Three thousand camels were stolen, and again, all but one of the servants perished. Finally, here are verses 18–19:

While he was still speaking, another also came and said, "Your sons and daughters were eating and drinking wine in their oldest brother's house, and suddenly a great wind came from across the wilderness and struck the four corners of the house, and it fell on the young people, and they are dead; and I alone have escaped to tell you!"   (Job 1:18–19)

In this case, Job lost seven sons and three daughters. I always tell people that if the wind strikes all four corners of a house at one time, you can know that Satan is behind it. We need to take note of the fact that Satan has many more resources than most of us realize.

In Job 2, we see that, after all this, the devil came back to God.

*And the L*ORD *said to Satan, "From where do you come?" So Satan answered the L*ORD *and said, "From going to and fro on the earth, and from walking back and forth on it." Then the L*ORD *said to Satan, "Have you considered My servant Job, that there is none like him on the earth, a blameless and upright man, one who fears God and shuns evil? And still he holds fast to his integrity, although you incited Me against him, to destroy him without cause." So Satan answered the L*ORD *and said, "Skin for skin! Yes, all that a man has he will give for his life. But stretch out Your hand now, and touch his bone and his flesh, and he will surely curse You to Your face!" And the L*ORD *said to Satan, "Behold, he is in your hand, but spare his life." So Satan went out from the presence of the L*ORD*, and struck Job with painful boils from the sole of his foot to the crown of his head.*   (verses 2–7)

Those boils were like adding insult to injury. Incidentally, the above passage is clear evidence that Satan can be the cause of sickness. I am not saying that he is the only cause or that he is always the cause of sickness. But he is one cause of sickness.

Let's summarize what was eliminated in order for God to get His way with Job. Five hundred oxen, five hundred female donkeys, and all but one of the servants who looked after them. Seven thousand sheep and all but one of the shepherds who looked after them. Three thousand camels and all but one servant. And then, all of Job's children: seven sons and three daughters. All of these losses occurred with the permission of the Lord. Again, I have asked myself many times, "What was God after?" As I understand it, He intended to reveal Himself to Job, and He was preparing Job for this revelation.

God Revealing Himself to You

This account shows me that God estimates things differently than we do. Because one man was so important to Him, He was willing to sacrifice all those things. God is never unjust. He is never unrighteous. But He has an aim—a purpose—in all He does, one which we may not always understand.

I want to state this point clearly, because I think it may apply in a lesser measure to you. You might sometimes wonder, *Why has this happened in my life? Why have I had to go through these things? Why did God let this occur? Other people don't seem to have the same problems that I have.* (I'm sure you never feel like that!)

> **God has an aim, a purpose, in all He does, which we don't always understand.**

In many cases, the reason we go through difficulties is the same reason Job did. We have experienced nothing on the order of what Job experienced. Nevertheless, God has permitted us to go through all sorts of trials and other situations that we did not really welcome. These hardships and difficulties were tough to endure and not easy to understand. But the Lord allowed them because He wants to bring us to the place where He can reveal Himself to us.

The Results of Job's Experience

1. Job Maintained His Righteousness

Let's look now at the outcomes of Job's experience. First, in the midst of all his pressures and troubles, Job consistently maintained his righteousness. He said,

> But He [the Lord] *knows the way that I take; when He has tested me, I shall come forth as gold.* [That is a marvelous statement.] *My foot has held fast to His steps; I have kept His way and not turned aside. I have not departed from the commandment of His lips; I have treasured the words of His mouth more than my necessary food.* (Job 23:10–12)

All of Job's so-called friends tried to convince him that he must have done something wrong and therefore truly deserved what was coming upon him. Job emphatically rejected that assertion. Amazingly, God Himself bore testimony to Job's righteousness, and He did so even before Job's troubles began:

> *There was a man in the land of Uz, whose name was Job; and that man was blameless and upright, and one who feared God and shunned evil....Then the* LORD *said to Satan, "Have you considered My servant Job, that there is none like him on the earth, a blameless and upright man, one who fears God and shuns evil?"* (Job 1:1, 8)

> *Then the* LORD *said to Satan, "Have you considered My servant Job, that there is none like him on the earth, a blameless and upright man, one who fears God and shuns evil? And still he holds fast to his integrity, although you incited Me against him, to destroy him without cause."* (Job 2:3)

And then, at the end of it all—when Satan had been allowed to do everything except take Job's life—the Lord gave this testimony about him:

> *And so it was, after the LORD had spoken these words to Job, that the LORD said to Eliphaz the Temanite, "My wrath is aroused against you and your two friends, for you have not spoken of Me what is right, as My servant Job has. Now therefore, take for yourselves seven bulls and seven rams, go to My servant Job, and offer up for yourselves a burnt offering; and My servant Job shall pray for you. For I will accept him, lest I deal with you according to your folly; because you have not spoken of Me what is right, as My servant Job has."*
> (Job 42:7–8)

In spite of everything that had happened to Job, the Lord still said he was perfectly righteous. Yet, to Job's friends, God essentially said, "You religious hypocrites, with all your religious talk! You need to repent." But note that for Job himself, God did not demand repentance. Instead, He testified that Job was righteous.

2. Job Repented When He Came Face-to-Face with God's Holiness

Having God appear on the scene to declare Job righteous was an amazing occurrence. But we see a deeper principle of holiness in Job's attitude when he encountered God face-to-face. Here is what Job said to God after he'd had a personal revelation of Him:

> *Listen, please, and let me speak; You said, "I will question you, and you shall answer Me." I have heard of You by the hearing of the ear, but now my eye sees You. Therefore I abhor myself, and repent in dust and ashes.*
> (Job 42:4–6)

Here was a man who was righteous, according to God's own testimony. But when he came into the presence of the Lord, he said, *"I abhor myself."* What had he encountered? I believe he had seen something of the Lord's holiness, and, by contrast with His righteousness, Job had to repent. He had to humble himself. I believe that was the purpose of God in all His dealings with Job. Again, He was working to bring Job to the place where He could confront him with a revelation of Himself. To me, that makes the book of Job meaningful.

It also makes life meaningful for us. As I wrote earlier, what Job experienced may apply to your life and mine. Historically, the book of Job is the oldest book in the Bible. Isn't it interesting that the Bible starts out with a conundrum? It deals with this amazing question: Why does a man like Job have to suffer, in spite of all his righteousness, which was acknowledged by the Lord Himself?

We all go through a lot of difficult experiences. Many times, we do not understand what we are going through or why. You may have prayed, "Lord, why did You take my wife?" or "Why did my husband leave me?" or "Why have my children turned out to be such a disappointment?" When we go through times of suffering, we have many such issues with God.

But I believe God uses our difficult experiences to bring us to a place where we will know Him better and also be better qualified to serve Him. After Paul had been stoned in Lystra for preaching the gospel, he and Barnabas told the Christians, *"We must through many tribulations enter the kingdom of God"* (Acts 14:22). Any road that bypasses the tribulations does not lead to the kingdom of God.

Holiness Is the Impartation of God

In studying the Bible, I have come to the conclusion that the highest God has to offer us is the revelation of Himself. But we have to be prepared for that revelation. Many things have to be adjusted in us first. Our priorities may have to change before we can receive the revelation.

What is the revelation? It is His holiness. Job was a perfectly righteous man, by human standards. But when he had a revelation of the Lord, he said, *"I abhor myself, and repent in dust and ashes"* (Job 42:6). That is the difference between God's holiness and the best that we can do. That is why holiness is not a set of good works. Holiness is the impartation of God in whatever measure we can receive it.

Let me point out one additional truth from the book of Job:

> **Holiness is the impartation of God in whatever measure we can receive it.**

> *Now the LORD blessed the latter days of Job more than his beginning; for he had fourteen thousand sheep* [double the number he had previously], *six thousand camels* [double the number], *one thousand yoke of oxen* [double the number], *and one thousand female donkeys* [double the number]. *He also had seven sons and three daughters.* (Job 42:12–13)

Everything that came back to Job was doubled, with the exception of his children, whom he got back in the same number as before. This fact actually reveals a wonderful truth.

I remember when a dear friend of ours suddenly lost his eldest daughter in a boating accident. God spoke to him and said, "You haven't lost her. She's gone ahead." In the same way, Job had not lost his sons and daughters. He didn't need double restored to him. He received double when he got the same number.

You might be tempted to say, "Well, Job wasted a lot of energy on all the intercession he did for his family. (See Job 1:4–5.) His children were all wiped out in one catastrophe." But, again, they weren't wiped out. This truth is so important for us to realize. We have not lost our loved ones if they were in Christ. They have gone ahead of us. And, if we keep the faith, we will end up where they are. I said "if we keep the faith" because, personally—and this may be controversial—I don't take it for granted that I will get to heaven. I must fulfill the conditions until the last moment. But, by God's grace, I trust I will, and I trust you will, too. But don't take it for granted. Don't become casual or self-righteous about it.

Settling the Difficulties of Your Past

All that we have discussed in this chapter is in connection with the revelation of holiness. God's holiness cannot be explained, and it cannot be defined; it can only be revealed. And God can reveal Himself in His holiness only in the measure in which we are prepared for the revelation.

Again, you may have gone through trials you did not understand. Many times, you may have cried out to God, "Why?" I can't explain why. But it could well be that God was in all of those things because of His desire to bring you to the place where you can have a revelation of His holiness.

As we close this chapter, I believe it would be appropriate to spend just a little time letting God remind us of our pasts. Think of all you have gone through and the disappointments you have suffered. Then, ask God, "Lord, what did You have in mind that You allowed those things to happen?"

I would imagine there is no human being who has not experienced disappointments in life. Basically, I have had a very favored life. I have certainly had disappointments, too, but not many. However, I have learned to identify with others who have had bitter disappointments and trials they could not understand. I have to tell you that I cannot give you the answer for those kinds of experiences in your life. There is only one Person from whom you can get the answer, and that is the Lord.

But if you are willing to believe in His absolute righteousness and His unfailing love and mercy, then you can have a different perspective on the experiences that have troubled and tormented you. You can recognize that they may have been designed to bring you to an encounter with the Lord and a revelation of His holiness. Then, you can come out like Job—a victor.

8

DIVINE DISCIPLINE/ FULLNESS OF LIFE

As we continue to explore the purposes of God's discipline in relation to holiness, it will be helpful for us to keep our eyes on the goal. God wants us to experience life to the fullest (see John 10:10), and a vital step toward obtaining fullness of life is His discipline.

In that regard, let me cite a verse that is a wonderful Scripture to proclaim:

> *The fear of the LORD leads to life, and he who has it will abide in satisfaction; he will not be visited with evil.*
> (Proverbs 19:23)

How can you turn down something as good as that? Many Christians are intimidated by the idea of the fear of the Lord. Yet the fear of the Lord and the acceptance of His dealings with us will lead us to life in Him in the fullest measure.

Partakers of God's Holiness

If God requires holiness of us, it is only logical that He provides the means for us to achieve it. One way is through submission to His discipline, which He extends to us as a loving heavenly Father. We will look at various Scriptures in the book of Hebrews on this topic.

For consider Him [Jesus] *who endured such hostility from sinners against Himself, lest you become weary and discouraged in your souls. You have not yet resisted to bloodshed, striving against sin. And you have forgotten the exhortation which speaks to you as to sons: "My son, do not despise the chastening of the LORD, nor be discouraged when you are rebuked by Him; for whom the LORD loves He chastens, and scourges every son whom He receives." If you endure chastening, God deals with you as with sons; for what son is there whom a father does not chasten? But if you are without chastening, of which all have become partakers, then you are illegitimate and not sons. Furthermore, we have had human fathers who corrected us, and we paid them respect. Shall we not much more readily be in subjection to the Father of spirits and live?*   (Hebrews 12:3–9)

The key to life is to be in subjection to the *"Father of spirits."* If you are not in subjection to Him, you really cannot know life as He intends you to know it.

Legitimate Sons and Daughters

Let's revisit Hebrews 12:10, which compares God's discipline to the discipline of human parents:

For they [our human parents] *indeed for a few days chastened us as seemed best to them....*

That does not mean that human parents take pleasure in punishing their children. It simply means that they do it with the best understanding they have. Any of us would quickly acknowledge that, sometimes, human parents are not altogether wise or correct in their discipline. Nevertheless, they are usually doing the best they can.

The writer of Hebrews went on to say,

...but [God disciplines us] *for our profit, that we may*
be partakers of His holiness. (Hebrews 12:10)

Notice that the end purpose of all chastening and correction is *"that we may be partakers of* [God's] *holiness."* That is
the ultimate purpose of divine discipline. That is the end to
which God directs all His interventions and all His controls in
our lives.

I have met many Christians who have been believers for
fifteen or twenty years, and whose attitude is, "God doesn't
need to correct me any longer." Actually, God needs to correct
you and me until we have become partakers of His holiness. As
long as that purpose has not been fulfilled, we are subject to
chastening and correction.

Continuing with verse 11, we read,

Now no chastening seems to be joyful for the present,
but painful ["grievous," KJV]; *nevertheless, afterward*
it yields the peaceable fruit of righteousness to those
who have been trained by it.

The Greek word translated *"trained"* means "gymnastically
trained." It is as if you are being put through a rigorous athletic
program, and that involves discipline. It means going against your
body's resistance to effort and the pain of sore muscles. It means
enduring hardship. But the purpose is that you may develop
strength, endurance, agility, and high performance. Likewise,
although our training through chastening may be painful, the
purpose is that we may be partakers of God's holiness.

Holiness Is Not Optional

The passage of Scripture we have been looking at con-
cludes with these verses:

Therefore strengthen the hands which hang down,
and the feeble knees, and make straight paths for your

feet, so that what is lame may not be dislocated, but rather be healed. Pursue peace with all people, and holiness, without which no one will see the Lord.

(Hebrews 12:12–14)

According to this Scripture, holiness is not optional. It is a part of total salvation. Over the years, we Christians have given people a very wrong impression. At times, we have led people to believe that "getting saved" is all they need. If they want to go further and receive the baptism in the Spirit and get sanctified, that is a kind of optional postgraduate course. Yet those concepts are a complete misrepresentation of Scripture, for the Word of God says that without holiness, no one can see the Lord.

We have also given people a wrong impression that salvation is a kind of static condition. We have told them, in essence, "The best thing you can do to stay saved is to sit in church and be safe." Salvation is not a static condition, and anybody who hopes to be safe by sitting in church is actually very unsafe.

Salvation is a way of life. It is progressive, unfolding, continuing. Having been a Pentecostal preacher for years, I can make the following statement: Pentecostals and Baptists have often misled God's people as to the essence of salvation. Many good Fundamentalists and Pentecostals who call themselves "saved" are far from God's salvation at this time. You say, "I was saved in 1953." I reply to that, "God bless you, brother, but we're now living decades later. What's happened in the meanwhile?"

> **Salvation is a way of life. It is progressive, unfolding, continuing.**

If you have not grown spiritually since you entered into salvation, you are a monstrosity. If you have not made any progress, the word *saved* no longer fits you. Again, according to Scripture, the ultimate end to which we are moving, day by day, is the partaking of God's holiness.

I have wept inwardly over many dear brothers and sisters who have been chastened by God and have not acknowledged it, because their theology teaches them it doesn't happen. That is a tragedy, and it causes me deep concern. It is a serious matter not to submit to the chastening of the Lord.

Another Scripture that illustrates this principle is Proverbs 4:18:

> But the path of the just ["righteous" NASB, NIV] is like the shining sun, that shines ever brighter unto the perfect day.

If you are walking in the way of righteousness, the light on your path is getting brighter every day. If you are still walking in yesterday's light, you are a backslider today. There is no stopping place in God until you reach the final goal. And that goal, again, is to be *"partakers of His holiness"* (Hebrews 12:10).

Two Common Errors Regarding God's Discipline

Let us now explore in greater depth this question of why God disciplines us. Do you remember what the writer of Hebrews said about this?

> You have forgotten the exhortation which speaks to you as to sons: "My son, do not despise the chastening of the LORD, nor be discouraged when you are rebuked by Him; for whom the LORD loves He chastens, and scourges every son whom He receives."
> (Hebrews 12:5–6)

There are two common errors people make in their attitudes toward God's discipline. Some people despise the chastening of the Lord, saying, "I don't believe God would treat me like that, because God doesn't treat His children in that way. That's not from God. I don't believe it. I don't accept it."

Then, there are others who are discouraged by circumstances in their lives and say, "Well, if that's how God is going to treat me, I just don't have any hope. Why did I have to go through something like that? You mean God is behind it? I can't take that. It's too much. I'll just give up." They are saying, in effect, "I'll just lie down and let the devil walk all over me."

In contrast to those two errors in perspective, we need to remember that being chastened, corrected, or disciplined is evidence that we are true sons and daughters of God. If we are not disciplined, woe to us. God is not treating us as His children.

The writer of Hebrews also said that we had human fathers who disciplined us, and we gave them respect. Unfortunately, that is not often true today. I have observed that there are many fathers who do not discipline their children. By God's grace, I am the head of a large family. I have seen children grow up in all sorts of ways. And I would have to say that if you want your children to travel a difficult path through life, just spoil them. You can be sure that they will be misfits for most of their lives. Children without discipline will go through life believing that life will treat them like their parents have treated them. But life does not play that game. Life operates by different rules.

The first thing that all children need is love. The second is discipline. Either one without the other is ineffective. It causes me great concern when I see how some parents are setting their children up for a difficult life through lack of loving discipline.

How to Respond to God's Discipline

In Hebrews 12:12–13, we see how we ought to respond when we are chastened, or disciplined, by the Lord:

Therefore strengthen the hands which hang down, and the feeble knees, and make straight paths for your feet, so that what is lame may not be dislocated, but rather be healed.

> **A lot of people waste time rebuking the devil when they should be submitting to God.**

In so many words, these verses tell us not to indulge in self-pity. The first time I got involved with a situation in which demons that were being cast out of someone named themselves, the third demon named itself as "Self-pity." When I heard that, it was like a book was opened to me. I thought, *Now I understand why so many people never get free. It's because they are tied down by self-pity.* They may say, "Poor me. I shouldn't have to go through that. God is too good to let His children suffer like that. I've got to rebuke the devil." A lot of people waste time rebuking the devil when they should be submitting to God. The devil laughs at you if you rebuke him but have not met God's conditions. I think discipline is an opportunity to let God examine us. All I would say is, let's submit to divine examination.

My whole background is British, but I would regularly find myself overcome with grief at the spiritual condition of the United States. What is the spiritual response to that condition? Plain and simple, we need to humble ourselves before almighty God. David said, *"I humbled myself with fasting"* (Psalm 35:13). Nor do I believe we will experience the personal breakthroughs we seek without the practice of fasting. And I don't believe that a revival of any significance will come until God's people humble their souls with fasting. Humility through fasting is a wonderful tool, because pride is something endemic in the human heart. Every one of us has it. We are by nature proud. We are by nature arrogant. We are by nature self-assertive. We are by nature self-seeking. We are by nature self-centered. And we have to change. One way to deal with our self-assertive ego is to humble it by fasting.

I often think of a lawyer in Washington, D.C., who heard me teach on fasting. On a particular day, he decided to fast, and he had a miserable time. Whenever he went near a restaurant or any place that sold food, something urged him to go inside. At the end of the day (and having a good legal mind), he gave his stomach a talking-to, saying, "Stomach, you've made a lot of trouble for me today, and to punish you for that, I'm going to fast tomorrow." That is the way to deal with an unruly stomach.

The point of what I have been saying is that we need to take positive action. Rather than giving in to self-pity when we are disciplined by the Lord, we need to examine ourselves, accept the chastening, and take appropriate action to move forward in our relationship with the Lord.

The Importance of Examining Ourselves

I now want to deal more deeply with this important subject of examining ourselves in connection with discipline. As I pointed out earlier, many Christians have the attitude, "I've served the Lord for so long, and I have had so many results that I couldn't possibly need discipline." If you think you could not possibly need discipline, you need it.

Let's look at Paul's instructions about the Lord's Supper, which is the focal point of the whole Christian gospel.

> *For I received from the Lord that which I also delivered to you: that the Lord Jesus on the same night in which He was betrayed took bread; and when He had given thanks, He broke it and said, "Take, eat; this is My body which is broken for you; do this in remembrance of Me." In the same manner He also took the cup after supper, saying, "This cup is the new covenant in My blood. This do, as often as you drink it, in remembrance of Me."* ***For as often as you eat this bread and drink this cup, you proclaim the Lord's death till He comes***.
>
> (1 Corinthians 11:23–26, emphasis added)

What a wonderful privilege it is to proclaim the Lord's death. I don't want to impose this pattern on anybody, but because of our very mobile and unsettled life, Ruth and I would take the Lord's Supper together as a couple every morning. It gave us the daily privilege of proclaiming the Lord's death. Believers will not take the Lord's Supper forever, but only until He comes. However, Communion is a continual reminder to us that He is coming. And we are to go on observing it until He comes.

Paul followed the above verses with some very important truths, beginning in 1 Corinthians 11:27:

> *Therefore whoever eats this bread or drinks this cup of the Lord in an unworthy manner will be guilty of the body and blood of the Lord.*

That is an extremely serious statement. I would say you could alternatively translate the phrase *"will be guilty of..."* as "will be answerable for...." In other words, once we have taken the Lord's Supper, we have declared that we know that Jesus died and shed His blood for our redemption. After that, we are accountable for what we know.

Then, Paul said,

> *But let a man examine himself, and so let him eat of the bread and drink of the cup.*   (verse 28)

Examining oneself before taking Communion used to be a practice with certain denominations, and it was sometimes made very legalistic, but its basis was scriptural. I think every person who partakes of Communion should normally take at least a few moments to check on his or her spiritual condition. Communion is a very healthy spiritual practice in the sense that it brings you back to the place where you have to examine the state of your heart. We cannot just go on from day to day, casually assuming that everything is right between God and us, or between us and our fellow Christians. A good time to check on ourselves is whenever we take the Lord's Supper. So, Paul wrote,

> *But let a man examine himself, and so let him eat of the bread and drink of the cup. For he who eats and drinks in an unworthy manner eats and drinks judgment to himself, not discerning the Lord's body.*
>   (1 Corinthians 11:28–29)

If you partake of Communion in an unworthy manner, you are bringing judgment on yourself—no matter who you are or how many years you have been a Christian. There is no time limit. I have been a Christian for many years, and God still disciplines me. I have not yet reached the stage of maturity where I am immune to discipline.

Our Three Options

Paul provided additional reasons for us to examine ourselves.

> *For this reason many are weak and sick among you, and many sleep.*   (1 Corinthians 11:30)

"*Sleep*" refers to dying in an untimely manner. What was the reason? They failed to examine themselves; they failed to judge themselves. If we fail to evaluate our spiritual status, we may become weak, we may become sickly, and some of us may die prematurely. Some Christians have died prematurely for the very reason that they held a wrong attitude toward the Lord or toward their fellow Christians. Such an attitude is clearly dangerous and costly. What is the remedy?

> *If we would judge ourselves, we would not be judged.* [We would not fall under weakness, sickness, or untimely death.] *But when we are judged, we are*

chastened ["disciplined" NASB] *by the Lord, that we may not be condemned with the world.*

(1 Corinthians 11:31–32)

> **We should view Communion as a wonderful opportunity for an honest assessment of our spiritual condition.**

My logical mind tells me we have three options: (1) we judge ourselves and repent; (2) we are chastened by the Lord and repent; (3) we fail to repent, and we are judged along with the world.

I do not believe there are any other options. Those three choices confront us every time we take the Lord's Supper.

We should view Communion as a wonderful opportunity for self-judgment—an honest assessment of our spiritual condition—and never partake of it casually or carelessly. If we judge ourselves at that time, God doesn't have to do it. If we are convicted, the best action we can take is to repent. Then, we will not come under the Lord's judgment. But if we do not repent, we will come under the Lord's judgment. And if we do not repent at that time, then God will treat us as He treats the world. That is perfectly logical.

A Picture of Repentance

I believe repentance is one of the key responses needed for the problems confronting the church, and I want to give you my own definition, or picture, of repentance. Suppose you are traveling along a road in the wrong direction and approaching a cliff. Repentance is like putting on the brakes and stopping. But that alone is not enough. You need to turn around and start driving in the opposite direction.

Let me share a vivid personal experience in this regard. In 1991, through foolishness on my part and through neglecting medical instruction, I became sick with what was called SBE. I had no idea what that was, but they told me I had subacute bacterial endocarditis, an inflammation of the lining of the heart that is normally fatal. In fact, until antibiotics were discovered, there was no treatment for it.

Fortunately, I was under the care of a rather clever doctor who diagnosed it early enough, and I immediately began a program of six weeks of intravenous antibiotics.

The night before I was admitted to the hospital (though I did not know at the time I would be admitted), I was seeking the Lord. I said, "Lord, I've preached healing, I believe in healing, I've been healed, and I've seen others healed. Why am I not being healed?" It took me quite a while to understand the Lord's answer, because He didn't give me a verbal answer. He gave me only a series of pictures of my past life, and most of the pictures were in restaurants.

I would say that, at that time, I was a respectable Pentecostal or charismatic preacher, and I was in fellowship with very respectable Christian brothers. But nobody told me what I was doing wrong except the Lord. He showed me that I was very self-indulgent, and He revealed to me that self-indulgence is the opposite of self-control. You cannot practice both at the same time. But the Lord did not bludgeon me with this truth. He just gave me these little pictures. And, as I thought about them, I began to see. So, I said, "Lord, I understand what You are telling me."

When I realized what God was saying to me, I made a U-turn. I stopped and turned around, and, from that time on, I was driving in the opposite direction. I had a ways to go, but at least I was going in the right direction. When the Lord spoke to me, I believe I was about five yards away from disaster. I could have gone over the cliff and died. And, if I had died, I would not have been a lost soul. But I would have been a disqualified preacher.

Time for Action

Where are you right now, spiritually? Do you, like most of us, need to confess to God the sin of carnality, of self-indulgence? Paul said, *"The flesh lusts against the Spirit, and the Spirit against the flesh..."* (Galatians 5:17). The result is that you cannot do all the things you want to. *"And these are contrary to one another, so that you do not do the things that you wish"* (verse 17). Are you striving to do certain things for God? If so, your flesh is striving against the Spirit. Which is going to prevail? Your answer to that question represents a very important personal decision on your part.

> **What controls your life? Is it the desires of the flesh? Is it your appetite? Is it a desire to impress people?**

In all self-assessment and divine examination, we need to come to a point of acknowledgment. I would like you to consider for a moment what controls you and what controls your life. Is it the desires of the flesh? Is it your appetite? Is it a desire to impress people? If so, you need to make a U-turn, and you might as well make it right now. All I can do is encourage you to make the right decision. Brothers and sisters can pray for you, but you have to make the decision. That is the nature of the soul. The soul makes its own decisions. No one can make a decision for another person's soul.

Make a U-turn

In light of what we have covered in this chapter, you may want to make an acknowledgment of what you see to be true about yourself, such as the following: "I am judging myself, and I realize I am very carnal. In many ways, I am motivated and controlled by the desires of my flesh. I see the need to make a U-turn—to stop, turn around, and proceed in the opposite direction."

If that is your condition, as well as your decision here and now, I invite you to acknowledge your condition and tell the Lord of your need. You can do so by praying the following prayer:

> Lord Jesus, I acknowledge that I have been controlled by fleshly, carnal desires. I realize I have grieved You. I have grieved and quenched Your Spirit. I am sorry, and I repent. I come to the place where I make a U-turn. I stop right now, and, by Your grace, Lord, and with Your help, I turn around. And, from this time forward, I will proceed in the opposite direction. I will no longer be ruled by my body. I take dominion over my body in the name of Jesus, and I bring it into subjection to the Spirit of God. In Jesus' name, amen.

Now, begin to thank and worship the Lord, remembering our passage from Hebrews, that God disciplines us...

> *...for our profit, that we may be partakers of His holiness. Now no chastening seems to be joyful for the present, but painful; nevertheless, afterward it yields the peaceable fruit of righteousness to those who have been trained by it. Therefore strengthen the hands which hang down, and the feeble knees, and make straight paths for your feet, so that what is lame may not be dislocated, but rather be healed.*
> (Hebrews 12:10–13)

9

SPIRITUAL BEAUTY

As we move forward in the theme of holiness, let us note this interesting fact: Holiness in the spiritual realm corresponds to beauty in the natural realm. In other words, the trait in the spiritual realm that is comparable to what we acknowledge as beauty in the physical body is holiness. Anybody who cares about beauty cares about holiness. Simply put, holiness is spiritual beauty.

"The Beauty of Holiness"

Let's look at a few statements in Scripture that bear out this truth, beginning with Psalm 93:5:

Your testimonies are very sure; holiness adorns Your house, O LORD, forever.

Please remember that the house of the Lord is not a church building; it is the people of God. In all generations, holiness is the aspect that adorns God's people, that suits them, that makes them look their best. Holiness is also what God requires in His house.

Next, *"the beauty of holiness"* is a phrase that is repeated several times throughout the Scriptures, including the following verses:

Oh, worship the LORD in the beauty of holiness! Tremble ["fear" KJV] before Him, all the earth.   (Psalm 96:9)

Give unto the LORD the glory due to His name; worship the LORD in the beauty of holiness. (Psalm 29:2)

I have been among many different kinds of Christians, and I find that, sometimes, the people who outwardly have very little to commend them have a higher degree of holiness. For example, I have known one or two Down's syndrome children. In a sense, they are simple. But when it comes to knowing God in their own way, they know Him much better than most of us. They have the inner beauty of holiness, even though it is accompanied by outward anomalies, such as physical weakness or distortion. If I had to choose (though God has not required me to), I would rather have the inner beauty of holiness than any kind of elegance, strength, or power. I earnestly desire that beauty for others and for myself, because the worship God accepts is worship that is beautified by holiness in the worshipper.

> **I would rather have the inner beauty of holiness than any kind of elegance, strength, or power.**

God's Beautiful Army

Psalm 110 gives us a unique, robust picture of God's people at the close of this age. It is a picture of the church as it emerges after centuries of darkness, human tradition, and error. The church that God is bringing forth will be a bride fit to meet the Bridegroom, Jesus. We see a depiction of this church in the third verse of Psalm 110, but let us begin by looking at the first two verses:

The LORD said to my Lord, "Sit at My right hand, till I make Your enemies Your footstool." The LORD shall send the rod of Your strength out of Zion. [Zion is the gathered company of God's people.] *Rule in the midst of Your enemies!*   (Psalm 110:1–2)

We know that *"my Lord"* in the above passage refers to Jesus; this portion of the Scriptures was interpreted by Jesus Himself. (See, for example, Matthew 22:41–45.) It is a picture of what Jesus is doing now. His enemies are still around; they still oppose. But He is ruling in the midst of His enemies out of the gathering of His people. And the rod of His strength, His authority, is going forth out of Zion.

Then, in Psalm 110:3, comes the description of God's people at the close of this age. It reads as follows in the King James Version:

Thy people shall be willing [the real meaning is "willing offerings," totally dedicated offerings, laid on the altar of God's holiness] *in the day of thy power, in the beauties of holiness from the womb of the morning: thou hast the dew of thy youth.*

If there is anything that appeals to me with its beauty, it is the sight of the sun rising on fresh green foliage and grass. As the sun rises, every little drop of dew begins to shine and sparkle in the sunlight. That is what holiness is like in the spiritual realm. God's people are coming out of the *"womb of the morning"* in the *"beauties of holiness"* for this last great manifestation of His glory and His power in His people.

Adorned in Holiness

Finally, let us turn to the New Testament to examine a very beautiful passage in 1 Peter that is directed specifically to Christian women. Let me just say that I think some preachers tend to overdo what the Bible teaches to women, without dwelling on what the Bible teaches to men. Understandably, some ladies tend to have a negative reaction to that oversight. I'm going to be careful not to make that mistake here. This verse speaks about the adorning of true saintly women.

> *Do not let your adornment be merely outward; arranging the hair, wearing gold, or putting on fine apparel....* (1 Peter 3:3)

Although I believe that every Christian has an obligation to be neat, clean, and acceptable in his or her appearance, that is not what really matters. Verses 4 and 5 make that fact clear:

> *...rather let it be the hidden person of the heart, with the incorruptible beauty of a gentle and quiet spirit, which is very precious in the sight of God. For in this manner, in former times, the holy women who trusted in God also adorned themselves.*

There is an adornment of holiness that is in the hidden person, in the heart. It is a *"gentle and quiet spirit."* Bystanders may not always appreciate it, but, in the sight of God, it is extremely precious.

Do you want to be regarded in that way by the Lord? If that is your desire, why not pray the following prayer as we conclude this chapter?

> **An adornment of holiness is a *"gentle and quiet spirit."***

Father, I thank You that this message about holiness in Your Word is so clear, so penetrating, so unambiguous. I pray that I will be open to the truth, that I will not turn away from it, and that I will not resist the Spirit of grace. I pray that when the Spirit speaks to me of holiness, I will be willing to listen and to humble myself. I know, Lord, that You are pleased to dwell with the humble and the contrite. I pray for Your people, for myself and for others, that as You look upon us from this day forward, You may see us in the beauty of holiness. And I will be careful, Lord, to give You the praise and the glory. In the name of Jesus, amen.

10

GOD'S PROVISION FOR HOLINESS

In previous chapters, we have examined the nature of the holiness of God—the unique aspect of God's character that is without parallel anywhere in creation. We have also noted the fact that God requires holiness in His people, and that, when God requires something of us, He makes it possible for us to fulfill His command. God has made provision for us to be partakers of His total nature, of His holiness. That truth is the basis of this chapter, and it is of great importance that we take hold of it.

A Multiplying Life

Let us begin by looking at 2 Peter 1:2–4 in the King James Version, which is a very good translation of the passage, although the English is somewhat elaborate. I will try to simplify it and also make it a little more up-to-date as I expound on the verses.

As an interesting side note, although the apostle Peter was a fisherman, and the apostle Paul was essentially a student and a theologian, when it comes to their writings, the language of Peter is much more elaborate than the language of Paul. My personal opinion is that, out of all the early church preachers, the outstanding preacher was not Paul but Peter. Paul was not a preacher. He said in 2 Corinthians 10:10 that his enemies criticized him because *"his bodily presence is weak, and his speech contemptible.*" But when you read the writings of Peter, you realize he must have been something of an orator. We find that quality in the passage we are going to look at now.

The Christian Life Is Not Static

Grace and peace be multiplied unto you through the knowledge of God, and of Jesus our Lord....

(2 Peter 1:2 KJV)

Let's note again that the Christian life is not a static condition in which you get into salvation and simply sit there. The Christian experience is a life of growth, increase, and multiplication. Frankly, if there is no growth, increase, or multiplication in your spiritual experience, I question whether you are in salvation at all.

> **The impartation of grace and peace from God is continually increasing.**

There is not one thing God has created that just remains static—unmoved and unchanged. Clearly, the believer in Christ is the summit of God's creation. So, if there ever should be unfolding growth, increase, and progress, it should be in the life of the Christian believer. This is what Peter was indicating here when he said, *"Grace and peace be multiplied unto you...."* That impartation of grace and peace from God is continually increasing.

Everything Depends on Knowing God and Jesus

Next, Peter said, *"...through the knowledge of God, and of Jesus our Lord"* (2 Peter 1:2 KJV). Everything is contained in knowing God and Jesus Christ. Jesus said elsewhere that to know the true God is eternal life. (See John 17:3.) I pointed out earlier that, in relation to holiness, a person can have no conception of what holiness means until he begins to know God. Everything we are speaking about here is wrapped up in knowing God and Jesus Christ in a direct and personal way.

We see the outworking of knowing God in 2 Peter 1:3–4:

According as his divine power hath given unto us all things that pertain unto life and godliness, through the knowledge of him that hath called us to glory and virtue: whereby are given unto us exceeding great and precious promises: that by these ye might be partakers of the divine nature, having escaped the corruption that is in the world through lust. (KJV)

Four Truths about God's Provision

There are four statements in the above passage that are of tremendous importance. Two statements are found in verse 3, and two are found in verse 4.

1. Full provision has already been given through God's power.

The first statement is that "[God's] *divine power hath given unto us all things that pertain unto life and godliness...*" (2 Peter 1:3 KJV). Notice, above all, the tense that is used. *Tense* refers to the form of verb, which shows the time of the action. It is not that God *will give*, but that He *has given*. God has already given us all we will ever need for this life and for the next. For time and for eternity, God has made complete, total provision by His power. It is essential that we grasp this truth.

2. Provision comes through acknowledging Christ.

The second part of 2 Peter 1:3 says, "*...through the knowledge of him* [Jesus Christ] *that hath called us to glory and virtue...*" (KJV). Where the King James Version says "*knowledge,*" the word in the original Greek actually means "acknowledging." In other words, our capacity to move forward in the things of God comes in proportion to the degree that we acknowledge Jesus Christ.

Let me state here that the church is not united by discussing doctrine. In fact, experience in history confirms that the more we discuss doctrine, the more divided we become. The church is united by acknowledging Jesus Christ. Paul said, *"Till we all come in the unity of the faith, and of the knowledge of the Son of God"* (Ephesians 4:13 KJV). Again, the Greek word for *"knowledge"* means "acknowledging." In other words, we move into the unity of the faith in proportion to the degree that we acknowledge the Lord Jesus Christ.

Quite plainly, every aspect of true Christian doctrine is an aspect of Jesus Christ and His ministry. You come into salvation through acknowledging Jesus as the Savior. You come into healing through acknowledging Jesus as the Healer. You come into the baptism in the Holy Spirit through acknowledging Jesus as the Baptizer. You come into deliverance through acknowledging Jesus as the Deliverer. Progress in the Christian life and unity among believers are not achieved by isolating doctrines and disputing about them but by acknowledging the Lord Jesus Christ for who He is. The more completely we acknowledge Him, the more we are united in Him and the more we develop in our own spiritual experiences. The second part of 2 Peter 1:3, therefore, confirms the truth that we enter into God's provision through the acknowledging of Jesus Christ.

3. The provision is in the promises of God.

Second Peter 1:4 states the actual means by which we enter into what God has provided. The first part of this verse says, *"...whereby are given unto us exceeding great and precious promises"* (KJV). The provision of God is in His promises. This is a tremendously important truth for us to realize.

The total provision for all believers is in the promises of God. I have developed a little slogan that I would like you to read out loud. Read it to yourself first, and then say it out loud, because you will remember it that way: "The provision is in the promises."

Proclaim it again, so that you will remember it: "The provision is in the promises."

4. As we appropriate God's promises, we partake of His nature and escape the world's corruption.

Let's look now at the latter part of 2 Peter 1:4, which clearly states what happens when we appropriate the promises of God. You may classify it as a single result or a double result; it doesn't matter. But the first result of appropriating the promises that Peter cited is that *"ye might be partakers of the divine nature..."* (KJV). You actually begin to partake of the very nature of God Himself.

Then, at the end of verse 4, Peter said, *"...having escaped the corruption that is in the world through lust"* (KJV). In proportion to how much we partake of God's nature, we escape the corruption of the old Adamic, or fallen, nature.

> **Sinful corruption and the divine nature are incompatible.**

Let's recognize this fact: sinful corruption and the divine nature are incompatible. Where sinful corruption prevails, there is nothing of the divine nature. Where the divine nature prevails, there can be no sinful corruption. So, again, in proportion to the degree to which we partake of the divine nature, we escape the corruption that we inherited from Adam.

Change Your Christian Experience

I hope I have made the essential truths that we have just examined very clear and that you understand them. Let's do a recap to make sure. If you can grasp these four facts, they can change your Christian experience:

1. First, full provision has already been made by God's power. God says He has made provision for all that you will ever need.

2. The provision comes through the progressive acknowledging of Jesus Christ. In proportion to the degree that we acknowledge Christ, we enter into God's provision.

3. The provision is in the promises of God's Word. (I hope you have already proclaimed this truth, applying it to yourself.)

4. As a result of appropriating God's promises in His Word and acknowledging Christ, two things follow in our personal experience. We are made partakers of the divine nature—of God's own nature—and, as we partake of God's own nature, we automatically escape the world's corruption.

11

LAND OF PROMISES

In the preceding chapter, we examined four truths that absolutely shape our Christian lives. In this chapter, I want to illustrate these truths from the Old Testament, or old covenant. We will begin our study in the book of Joshua, where we find a very clear illustration. Let us first look at the background to it.

Our Inheritance under a New Covenant

Under the old covenant, the inheritance God led His people into was the physical Promised Land, the land of Canaan. Under the new covenant, the inheritance God leads His people into is a land of promises. All the principles that applied under the old covenant apply equally under the new.

In the old covenant, the leader who brought God's people into the Promised Land was named Joshua. In the new covenant, the leader who brings His people into the land of promises is named Jesus. In Hebrew, *Jesus* and *Joshua* are the same word.

There are two books in the Old Testament that deal specifically with entering into the inheritance of God's people. The first of these is the book of Deuteronomy, which lays the basic principles for entering into and remaining in your inheritance. Then, the book of Joshua describes the actual experience of the children of Israel as they applied these principles and entered into their inheritance. If you read Deuteronomy and Joshua with that understanding, you will find that these books cast tremendous light upon your experience as you enter into and remain in your inheritance in Christ.

Joshua's Commission

After the death of Moses the servant of the LORD, it came to pass that the LORD spoke to Joshua the son of Nun, Moses' assistant, saying: "Moses My servant is dead. Now therefore, arise, go over this Jordan, you and all this people...." (Joshua 1:1–2)

> **Sometimes, there has to be a death before new life can come forth.**

Sometimes, there has to be a death before new life can come forth. Sometimes, one order has to terminate before a new order can develop. Moses was God's appointed leader to bring Israel out of Egypt. But God had told Moses very clearly that he would not be the one to bring God's people into their inheritance in the new land. (See Numbers 20:7–12.) Moses had to die before God's people could move in.

I believe there is a parallel situation in the church today. I trust I will not offend anyone by saying this, and I hope you will understand it in the right way, but I believe there has been a death in Christianity, and what has died is the institutional church. I am not saying the Baptist church has died, or the Pentecostal church, or the Episcopal church, or the Catholic church. I am saying the institutional church is dead. And I think we have probably mourned over it long enough.

As I see it, the institutional church is like Moses—it cannot take us, God's people, into the inheritance that God has appointed for us in this generation. We need to have new leadership, a new pattern, a new way of going forward. And I believe God is leading us into this new pattern in our modern times.

Israel was allowed thirty days to mourn over Moses. God is a psychologist. He knows that traumatic events shock people and that it takes them a while to adjust. Then, after the thirty days, He said to Joshua, in effect, "It's time to stop mourning and start moving. Moses is dead. That isn't the end of the world. In fact, it is the end of one phase and the beginning of a new phase."

Realizing the Promise

Let's look now at the principles that unfolded as Joshua was commissioned to lead God's people into their inheritance. The Lord said,

> *Moses my servant is dead. Now therefore, arise, go over this Jordan, you and all this people, to the land which I am giving to them; the children of Israel. Every place that the sole of your foot will tread upon I have given to you, as I said to Moses.*   (Joshua 1:2–3)

I want to point out two different tenses of the word *give* that were used by the Lord in the above passage. In verse 2, He said, *"The land which I **am giving** to them"*—present tense. He was giving them the land while He was speaking. But by verse 3, it had become the present perfect tense, which signifies something that has already taken place or been accomplished: *"Every place that the sole of your foot will tread upon I **have given** to you."*

From that moment onward, the entire land legally belonged to the Israelites, but they still had to appropriate it. And they did this by putting the soles of their feet on every area of the land. As they placed the soles of their feet upon every area, it became theirs experientially.

We need to recognize that there is a tremendous difference between legal possession and experiential possession. You have probably heard statements like this from other Christians:

"Brother, I don't need any experience beyond salvation. I don't need any second blessing. I don't need the baptism in the Holy Spirit. I got it all when I was saved." The answer is, "Yes, you did—legally. But not experientially."

Please forgive me for making these parallels, but I would say that if Joshua and the children of Israel had been Fundamentalists, they would have lined up on the east bank of the Jordan River with their arms folded and said, "We've got it all!" By the same token, if they had been Pentecostals, they would have crossed the Jordan, lined up on the west bank, and said, "We've got it all!" Regardless of which side of the Jordan they lined up on, the Canaanites would have been laughing at them because they knew who had the land in experience. Again, we need to recognize the difference between legal inheritance and experiential possession.

Israel had received the entire Promised Land legally from Joshua 1:3 onward. Legally, it was theirs forever. But not experientially. At least, not yet.

Putting Your Foot Down

> **All the promises are yours in Christ already. However, you must possess them experientially.**

This difference between legal and experiential possession is significant as well for us in the Christian life. As I said earlier, our inheritance is the land of promises. All the promises are yours in Christ already. (See 2 Corinthians 1:20.) However, you must put the soles of your feet upon them to possess them experientially.

Every step that the children of Israel took into their inheritance under the old covenant was contested by their enemies. Likewise, every step you take into your inheritance in Christ under the new covenant will be contested by your enemies. The enemies under the old covenant were Perizzites, Hittites, Hivites, Jebusites, Canaanites, Amorites, and a lot of other "-ites." And the "-ites" that will contest your progress under the new covenant are all the forces of Satan, including evil spirits and demons.

You have to set your face like flint (see Isaiah 50:7) and move into the land of promises, saying, "The Lord has given me this land, and I am putting my feet here. Satan, you move off!" Realize that Satan moves only when he is confronted with faith plus determination. If you try to confront him without those attributes, he will continue to hold on to your inheritance. Though you may possess it legally, you will not enjoy it in experience. Those are very important basic principles.

Seven Provisions for Becoming Partakers of God's Holiness

Now, we will begin to apply these principles to the truths of holiness. Let's review what we have already learned from the book of Hebrews, which says that God chastens, or disciplines, us *"for our profit, that we may be partakers of His holiness"* (Hebrews 12:10). Recall that Peter used the phrase *"partakers of the divine nature"* (2 Peter 1:4). The writer of Hebrews talked about our being partakers of one particular aspect of the divine nature—God's holiness. But it is the same for all aspects of the divine nature. The principles of provision I am now unfolding in relation to holiness actually apply in many other areas of the Christian life with little to no modification. For instance, almost exactly the same principles would apply for healing.

How can we partake of the divine nature? What is God's provision for holiness? We will divide this provision into seven parts, so that we can get the clearest possible understanding of each aspect. In studying the New Testament, I have found that there are seven provisions of God that we need in order to partake of our inheritance of holiness:

1. Jesus Christ

2. The Cross (the place of Jesus' sacrifice)

3. The Holy Spirit

4. The Blood of Jesus

5. The Word of God

6. Our Faith

7. Our Works (the actions whereby we express our faith)

We will cover these seven provisions of God in relation to holiness in more detail in the next chapter.

12

SEVEN ASPECTS OF GOD'S PROVISION FOR HOLINESS

W e will now work through the seven aspects of God's provision needed for us to partake of our inheritance of holiness in God, as listed at the end of the previous chapter.

1. Jesus Christ

The first aspect is Jesus Christ. We have already seen that it is through acknowledging Jesus Christ that we enter into total provision: "[God's] *divine power hath given unto us all things that pertain unto life and godliness, through the knowledge* [acknowledging] *of him* [Jesus Christ] *that hath called us to glory and virtue*" (2 Peter 1:3 KJV). In respect to holiness, or sanctification, this truth was also stated clearly by the apostle Paul:

> *To the church of God which is at Corinth, to those who are sanctified in Christ Jesus, called to be saints* [holy ones].   (1 Corinthians 1:2)

It is plain from this passage that our sanctification is in Christ Jesus. Outside of Christ Jesus, there is no provision for sanctification. It all begins with Him. At the end of that chapter, Paul said even more clearly,

> *But of Him* [God the Father] *you are in Christ Jesus, who became for us wisdom from God; and righteousness and sanctification and redemption.*   (verse 30)

To every believer, God the Father has made Jesus wisdom, righteousness, sanctification (holiness), and redemption—these four essentials. They are all in Christ. Every blessing God has for us comes to us through Jesus Christ.

Let's look at two additional Scriptures that line up with this thought:

> *For the law was given through Moses, but grace and truth came through Jesus Christ.*　　　(John 1:17)

> *He who did not spare not His own Son, but delivered Him up for us all, how shall He not with Him also freely give us all things?*　　　(Romans 8:32)

With Christ, it is *"all things."* Without Christ, it is "no thing." Our entire inheritance is in Jesus Christ alone.

2. The Cross

The second provision for holiness is in the cross. The author of Hebrews summed up this idea in one tremendous verse:

> *For by one offering* [sacrifice] *He has perfected forever those who are being sanctified.*　　　(Hebrews 10:14)

The offering, or the sacrifice, is the death of Jesus Christ on the cross. In the above Scripture, the tenses in the original Greek are extremely important, because there is a clear distinction between them. The first part of the verse says, *"For by one offering He **has perfected**...."* This is stated in the perfect tense, which denotes something that is finished, complete; something that cannot be touched, added to, or changed. But the second part of the verse says this: *"...forever those who **are being sanctified**."* Sanctification is a continuing, progressive process.

Many people have misunderstood the relationship between the perfect sacrifice and the continuing appropriation of the sacrifice. As a result, some false ideas about instant holiness have sprung up. For myself, I don't believe in instant holiness any more than I believe in "instant" coffee! If you want real coffee, you have to make it in a percolator. And if you want any real experience with God, there is a process of "percolation." If you bypass the percolator, the results will be disappointing.

If you can develop a mental picture of the cross, you will be able to visualize its great significance. Picture in your mind the cross as a kind of vertical intervention of God in human history and on every individual human life. The main beam of the cross is vertical; it comes down from God and bisects human life. It is one perfect sacrifice. That can never be changed. On the other hand, the horizontal beam represents human life, which is continually unfolding. After the cross has come into our lives, there is a progressive appropriation of what it has made available to us.

So, what Jesus has done on the cross is perfect and eternal, but our appropriation of it is not instantaneous and complete. We are progressively being sanctified.

People who believe that sanctification ought to be instantaneous but do not receive it instantly tend to experience self-condemnation. Or, they think something has gone wrong and God is not doing what He promised to do. What they need to understand is that God's part is complete, while our appropriation is progressive. It is very important to see this aspect of holiness because it gets rid of a lot of misunderstanding and prevents feelings of condemnation in our Christian experience.

> **We need to remember that our appropriation of sanctification is progressive, not instant.**

3. The Holy Spirit

The third factor in God's provision is the Holy Spirit. Let's begin with the part the Holy Spirit plays in sanctification. The first Scripture we will look at in this regard is 1 Corinthians 6:11, which begins, *"And such were some of you...."*

If you want to know what Paul was referring to by *"such,"* you need to read the two previous verses. It is not very pleasant reading. It refers to fornicators, idolaters, adulterers, homosexuals, sodomites, thieves, coveters, drunkards, revilers, and extortionists. These Corinthian believers did not all come from the most refined social backgrounds. *"Such,"* Paul said, *"were some of you. But..."* (verse 11). How I thank God for that *"but"*! Don't you? It represents a cutoff from the past and the beginning of something new.

> *But you were washed, but you were sanctified, but you were justified in the name of the Lord Jesus and by the Spirit of our God.*   (1 Corinthians 6:11)

The administrator of Christ's grace is the Holy Spirit. So, the basis of the provision is the cross. The One who administers the cross's benefits in our lives is the Spirit. And one of the benefits He administers is sanctification.

Let's now look at another verse that we will refer to from this point on:

> *But we are bound to give thanks to God always for you, brethren beloved by the Lord, because God from the beginning chose you for salvation through sanctification by the Spirit and belief in the truth.*
> (2 Thessalonians 2:13)

If we focus on the second part of that verse, we get the following tremendous statement: *"God from the beginning chose you for salvation through sanctification by the Spirit and belief in the truth."* Sequentially, I believe this is the process through which we enter into salvation: (1) God chooses in eternity, *"from the beginning."* (2) In time, the Holy Spirit begins to sanctify us—to set us apart, to draw us—to the place where we receive a revelation of God. (We will examine this concept more fully in later chapters.) (3) The Holy Spirit's sanctifying work brings us to believe the truth of God's Word. (4) In believing the truth, we enter into salvation, or we are brought into salvation.

It is important to understand that no matter how people may feel about it, this is what the Bible says. The sanctifying work of the Holy Spirit begins before we come to salvation. Actually, if the Holy Spirit did not begin the work, we would never come to salvation.

We find basically the same outline as the one I gave above in 1 Peter. Speaking to believers in Christ, the apostle Peter said,

> *To the...elect [*"chosen" NASB*] according to the foreknowledge of God the Father, in sanctification of the Spirit, for obedience and sprinkling of the blood of Jesus Christ.* (1 Peter 1:1–2)

Note that Peter did not merely speak about God's choice, but he also spoke about God's foreknowledge, which, in logical terms, precedes God's choice. So, in eternity, we have this scenario: God foreknows us, and, on the basis of His foreknowledge, He chooses us. In time, the Holy Spirit begins His sanctifying work in our lives and brings us to the place of obedience to God's Word and the gospel. When we obey the Word, then the blood of Jesus Christ is sprinkled upon us in salvation, cleansing, and separation.

Let's look closely at one basic fact: The blood is sprinkled upon only the obedient. The disobedient do not have access to the blood of Jesus. This principle applies all through the Christian life. We see it in 1 John 1:7, which says, *"If we* [continually] *walk in the light as He is in the light, we* [continually]

> **Walking in the light means walking in obedience to the light of God's Word.**

have fellowship one with another, and the blood of Jesus Christ His Son [continually] *cleanses us from all sin."* There is a conditional aspect to this verse. Being kept clean by the blood is contingent upon walking in the light. Walking in the light means walking in obedience to the light of God's Word, which is a lamp to our feet and a light to our paths. (See Psalm 119:105.)

Please remember this truth: Access to the blood of Jesus depends upon our obedience. As soon as we become disobedient, we forfeit the right of access to the blood until we repent.

4. The Blood of Jesus

The fourth aspect of God's provision for holiness is the blood of Jesus. Let's look again at 1 Peter 1:2. The Holy Spirit, by His sanctifying work, brings us to obedience, and through our obedience, the Holy Spirit ministers to us the blood of Jesus. The blood of Jesus separates us from our old, sinful pasts and backgrounds. As we will discuss further in the next chapter, we come to the "blood line" at the cross. Crossing the blood line, we pass out of Satan's kingdom and into God's kingdom in Christ. That is the point of transition.

We will look now at two other Scriptures that speak about the sanctifying power of the blood of Jesus. The first is Hebrews 10:29:

> *Of how much worse punishment* [than a transgressor under the law of Moses], *do you suppose, will he be thought worthy who has trampled the Son of God underfoot, counted the blood of the covenant by which he was sanctified a common* ["unholy" KJV] *thing, and insulted the Spirit of grace?*

This Scripture tells us, first of all, that the believer is sanctified through the blood of the covenant. To me, this verse also makes it clear that it is possible to lose your sanctification. By a deliberate rejection of Jesus Christ and His shed blood, you forfeit the sanctification that was made available through the blood.

You will remember that under the old covenant, in the ceremony of the Passover lamb, the blood of the lamb was sprinkled on the lintels and on the two side posts of the door but not on the threshold. Because this blood was sacred, no one was permitted to walk upon it. The above verse sets up a hypothetical situation in which somebody turns and deliberately tramples underfoot Jesus Christ and His blood. Such a person who does this has *"insulted the Spirit of grace,"* which means he or she has deliberately slighted and rejected the Holy Spirit. Frighteningly, such a person has passed beyond any possibility of recall to repentance.

What I have just covered is obviously not the main theme of this section. However, the statement above reminds us that we need to be extremely careful in our attitudes toward the blood of Jesus and toward the Holy Spirit. If a person ever does count the blood of Jesus an unholy thing, that person has insulted the Holy Spirit. Conversely, if a person insults the Holy Spirit, that person forfeits the right of access to the blood. The blood and the Spirit go very closely together.

Hebrews 13:12 is yet another Scripture about the sanctifying operation of the blood of Jesus:

> *Therefore Jesus also, that He might sanctify the people with His own blood, suffered outside the gate* [on the cross].

One purpose for Jesus' death on the cross was to provide the blood that He shed there, by which God's people might be sanctified—set apart for God and for their inheritance in Christ.

5. The Word of God

The next factor in this process is the Word of God. The Word follows the blood. A beautiful Scripture about the sanctifying power of God's Word is found in the seventeenth chapter of John. This chapter contains the great High Priestly Prayer of Christ on behalf of His disciples and all His followers. Let us read a portion of this prayer before coming to the particular verse I want to share with you:

> *I do not pray that You should take them out of the world, but that You should keep them from the evil one* [the devil]. *They are not of the world, just as I am not of the world.*　　　　　　　　　　　　(John 17:15–16)

The true believer is in the world but not of the world. (See also verses 11, 14.) Mere physical separation from the world in a convent or a monastery, for example, would not resolve this problem. It is a spiritual problem and cannot be solved merely by a physical separation. Jesus laid out the solution in the next verse, which contains these beautiful words:

> *Sanctify them by Your truth. Your word is truth.*
> 　　　　　　　　　　　　　　　　　　　　(verse 17)

I prefer to say, "Your word is *the* truth." As someone has said, "Some things are true, but they are not *the truth*." You may have a toothache and be in pain. That is truth. But it is not *the* truth, which is, *"By His stripes we are healed"* (Isaiah 53:5).

Some things are true now, but they will change. However, what is in God's Word is the truth, and it never changes. (See, for example, Psalm 119:89, 160.) And it is the truth of God's Word that sanctifies the believer in Jesus Christ. This fact is also stated in 2 Thessalonians 2:13, the passage I mentioned earlier and said that we would refer to frequently:

God from the beginning chose you for salvation through sanctification by the Spirit and belief in the truth.

The Holy Spirit brings you to believe the truth of God's Word, and that is a further phase of your sanctification.

I believe the greatest single Scripture passage on the sanctifying role of the Word is Ephesians 5:25–27. This passage introduces a parallel using the relationship between husband and wife and the relationship between Christ and His bride, the church:

> *Husbands, love your wives, just as Christ also loved the church and gave Himself for her, that He might sanctify and cleanse her with the washing of water by the word, that He might present her to Himself a glorious church, not having spot or wrinkle or any such thing, but that she should be holy and without blemish.*

Here we have the interrelationship between the blood and the Word. We see that Christ loved the church and gave Himself for her as the substitutionary sacrifice upon the cross, shedding His blood (that was the redemption price) to redeem the church. But He redeemed the church for this purpose: so that He might thereafter *"sanctify and cleanse her with the washing of water by the word."*

It is vital for us to understand that redemption through the blood is God's gateway into cleansing and sanctification by the water of the Word. The process of making us holy is not completed through

The process of making us holy is completed through the continual sanctifying and cleansing operation of the Word.

redemption by the blood; it must be completed through the continual sanctifying and cleansing operation of the Word in the life of every believer.

The conclusion of the two operations is stated in Ephesians 5:27:

> *That He* [Christ] *might present her to Himself a glorious church, not having spot or wrinkle or any such thing, but that she should be holy and without blemish.*

It is my firm conviction that no believer will qualify to be a member of the bride of Christ, a part of the glorious church that is to be presented to Jesus Christ, unless he or she regularly submits to the discipline, the cleansing, and the sanctifying of the Word of God. The experience of having entered into redemption through the cross does not, in itself, constitute adequate preparation for that great and glorious day when we are to be presented to Jesus Christ as a chaste and spotless bride.

The water of the Word has an essential part to play in making us ready for that great presentation. I find that many believers who think they are redeemed by the blood are very slack and careless in their attitudes toward the sanctifying process of the Word in their lives. I am deeply concerned about the present state of Christians who really pay very little attention to the Scriptures.

It may be true that the majority of Christians hardly ever read the Bible. Very few have ever read the whole Bible right through. Consequently, they are totally unaware of certain biblical principles. It is exciting to have the gifts of the Holy Spirit and manifestations of God's power, but those are no substitute for knowing the Word of God and apprehending its promises.

I have to say, the Bible's promises are breathtaking. For example, we *"may be partakers of the divine nature, having escaped the corruption that is in the world through lust"* (2 Peter 1:4). Let me ask you: How much have you partaken of the divine nature? How far have you really escaped the corruption that is in the world through lust? It is up to you to answer these questions.

I cannot answer them for you. But being holy as God is holy should be a key focus of our lives, and that requires the cleansing, sanctifying process of the Word in our lives.

Let's take one more look at the passage in Ephesians:

> *Husbands, love your wives, just as Christ also loved the church and gave Himself for her, that He might sanctify and cleanse her with the washing of water by the word.* (Ephesians 5:25–26)

Jesus makes the church what He intends it to be through the washing of water by the Word. Without that work, the church could never become what God has purposed. There is no substitute for the Word of God and its role of cleansing.

As we conclude this section, let's look at 1 John 5. Speaking about Jesus, John said,

> *This is He who came by water and blood; Jesus Christ; not only by water, but by water and blood. And it is the Spirit who bears witness, because the Spirit is truth.... And there are three that bear witness on earth: the Spirit, the water, and the blood; and these three agree as one.* (verses 6, 8)

Jesus came not only as the teacher of the Word (*"by water"*), but also as the substitutionary sacrifice (*"by blood"*). God's provision incorporates both the blood shed on the cross and the sanctifying water of the Word. As the believer comes first to the blood and then to the Word, the Spirit of God in the believer's heart bears witness to both the blood and the Word.

In fact, verse 8 says there are three witnesses on earth that bear testimony to Jesus Christ and agree as one in Him. These three witnesses to Jesus should be present in the life of every believer: the witness of the blood, the witness of the water of the Word, and the Holy Spirit, who bears witness to the blood and to the Word.

6. Our Faith

In the final two sections of this chapter, we will examine the part we have to play in appropriating the sanctifying means that God has put at our disposal. We have dealt with these aspects: Jesus Christ, the cross, the Holy Spirit, the blood of Jesus, and the Word of God. Now, we come to our faith and our works.

> **Our faith is the funnel through which God's grace and blessing can be poured into our lives.**

All that God has provided through Christ must be appropriated by the believer through personal faith. Our faith is the funnel through which God's grace and blessing can be poured into our lives. Unless we have the funnel of faith and have it turned in the right direction, we cannot receive all the provision God has made.

Let's look at two Scriptures that emphasize this point. First, we will return to the latter half of 2 Thessalonians 2:13:

> *God from the beginning chose you for salvation* [that is the purpose of God's choice, salvation] *through* [two processes:] *sanctification by the Spirit and belief in the truth.*

In the Greek, the word translated as *"belief"* in this verse is the same word that is translated almost exclusively as *"faith"* throughout the New Testament. There comes a time in our lives when our faith has to appropriate the truth of God's Word in order for us to enter into the provision of holiness that God has made.

There is another beautiful verse related to this theme—Acts 26:18—that I can never read without getting stirred up. God always seems to speak to me personally through this verse, in which the apostle Paul was speaking of his call as Jesus' apostle to the Gentiles. And this is how Jesus described Paul's purpose in bringing the gospel to the Gentiles:

...To open their eyes, in order to turn them from darkness to light, and from the power of Satan to God, that they may receive forgiveness of sins and an inheritance among those who are sanctified by faith in Me.
(Acts 26:18)

Don't let anyone ever tell you that Satan has no power, because that would be a silly thing to say. The Bible tells us that Satan has power. But, through the gospel, our eyes can be opened, and we can be turned from darkness to light, from the power of Satan to the power of God. When we so turn, we receive, first of all, forgiveness of sins. That is basic. Our first requirement is to have our sins forgiven, placing us in a position to relate to almighty God without the barrier of sin. Second, we receive an inheritance among those who are sanctified by faith in Him. The inheritance is reserved for those who are sanctified through their faith in Christ.

One other excellent Scripture in this regard is Colossians 1:12:

Giving thanks to the Father who has qualified us [made us capable] *to be partakers of the inheritance of the saints in the light.*

Notice that this inheritance is for the saints, or the holy ones—the ones who have been made holy by their faith in Jesus Christ. As Jesus said in His words to Paul, He intends to give His inheritance to those who are sanctified, set apart for God, by faith in Him.

7. Our Works

Finally, our faith must express itself in positive action. James 2:26 says that *"faith without works is dead."* Faith that does not express itself in action is dead faith. This same truth is stated specifically with regard

> **Our faith must express itself in positive action.**

to sanctification in 2 Corinthians 7:1, which we have examined in a previous chapter:

> *Therefore, having these promises, beloved, let us cleanse ourselves from all filthiness of the flesh and spirit, perfecting holiness in the fear of God.*

I pointed out earlier that the provision is in the promises. In this passage, Paul said that in light of the provision made available through the promises, it is up to us to do something— we have to apply the promises. We have to put our feet upon the land of our inheritance. We have to take it for ourselves.

Paul said, *"Let us cleanse ourselves."* God is not going to do it for us. He has made it possible for us to do it. Recall that, if we are to be holy, we must cleanse ourselves from two kinds of filthiness: first, from filthiness of the flesh, or the carnal sins, like drunkenness, immorality, swearing, and so on; and, second, from filthiness of the spirit, which is a far nastier expression of filthiness: involvement with Satan's supernatural realm, the occult. That filthiness comes to those who trespass in forbidden territory, with such things as Ouija boards, fortune-telling, horoscopes, astrology, séances, false prophecies, and Eastern cults and philosophies. All these practices contribute to filthiness of the spirit.

Let's look at one other Scripture that applies to all of God's provisions for us and in every area of our Christian experience regarding our need to respond to His initiative in our lives:

> *Therefore, my beloved, as you have always obeyed, not as in my presence only, but now much more in my absence, work out your own salvation with fear and trembling; for it is God who works in you both to will and to do for His good pleasure.* (Philippians 2:12–13)

God works in you; then, you have to work it out. If you don't work out what God works in, then God will not go on working in you.

I realize there are many principles and truths to absorb from this chapter. Why don't you ask the Lord to help you apply them to your life? You may do so by praying the following prayer:

Father, I give You praise and thanks that You have been with me as I have read through this chapter. I thank You for the fullness and completeness of Your provision, as I see it in Your Word. I pray, Lord, that I will not be slothful or careless or negligent in availing myself of Your provision. Please help me to be faithful and diligent to appropriate the holiness that You have made available to cleanse me from all filthiness of the flesh and the spirit. In Jesus' name I pray, amen.

13

HOW HOLINESS WORKS IN US

In this chapter, we will begin to see how the seven aspects of God's provision for holiness, as revealed in the Scriptures, actually work in our lives—how they enter our experience, and how we are to respond to each one. In other words, how do we apply the truth of all we have discovered so far in a practical, experiential way?

The Operation of God the Father in Eternity

Let's return to a passage we have discussed before. It comes from Peter's first epistle, where he was describing Christians:

> *To the...elect ["chosen" NASB] according to the foreknowledge of God the Father, in sanctification of the Spirit, for obedience and sprinkling of the blood of Jesus Christ.* (1 Peter 1:1–2)

Earlier, I pointed out through this verse that the first dynamic we encounter is God's foreknowledge, which is in eternity. On the basis of His foreknowledge, God chooses us in eternity. All of this happens before time even starts to roll. I have no problem believing that God knows all in advance. And if He knows all in advance, it is reasonable that He also chooses in advance on the basis of what He knows. This is what the Bible really teaches.

For another Scripture on this theme, let us turn to the book of Ephesians.

> *Blessed be the God and Father of our Lord Jesus Christ, who has blessed us with every spiritual blessing in the heavenly places in Christ, just as He chose us in Him before the foundation of the world* [again, this all happened before time began], *that we should be holy and without blame before Him in love....*
> (Ephesians 1:3–4)

Please notice that His choice is for us to be holy. In other words, His choice initiates our holiness. The next verse says this about God:

> *...having predestined us to adoption as sons by Jesus Christ to Himself, according to the good pleasure of His will.* (verse 5)

In the above verses, we find two events that happened in eternity: God chose, and He predestined. Added to these facts, we have the truth we discovered in 1 Peter 1:2 that He foreknew us. So, now we have three successive facts: God foreknew, He chose, and He predestined. The word *predestined* indicates that God arranged the circumstances of our lives in such a way that would allow His purposes to be fulfilled.

These realizations are further reinforced by the teaching of Romans 8. We will focus first on verse 29:

> *For whom He* [God] *foreknew, He also predestined to be conformed to the image of His Son, that He* [the Son, Jesus] *might be the firstborn among many brethren* [we are the brethren].

We see again that God foreknew, and then He predestined. If we put these three passages together, we get the same clear picture of God's operation in eternity. God the Father does three things: (1) He foreknows, (2) He chooses, and (3) He predestines.

The word *predestine* puts some people's backs up. They dislike this term because it is associated with a very narrow view of divine election that is unscriptural. It is important to establish the fact that God's choice, His election, is not arbitrary. It is not unreasonable. It is not unfair. God chooses us on the basis of His foreknowledge of us. He knows how we will respond to the situations in which He intends to place us, and He knows how we will respond to the call of the gospel when we hear it.

All of those actions happen in eternity, and it is essentially the prerogative of God the Father to take those steps. (Please note that I am not implying that the Son and the Spirit aren't involved in this process, because, of course, they are.)

The Operation of the Holy Spirit in Time

Next, we look at the operation of God (primarily by the Holy Spirit) in time. The Holy Spirit sanctifies. In this context, the word *sanctify* as an operation of the Holy Spirit means "to draw, to separate, and to reveal."

Let's return to 1 Peter 1:1–2, which is a key Scripture for all of this teaching on holiness:

> *To the...elect according to the foreknowledge of God the Father, in sanctification of the Spirit, for obedience and sprinkling of the blood of Jesus Christ.*

Notice where the sanctifying operation of the Holy Spirit is placed in the context. First, we read, *"To the...elect according to the foreknowledge of God the Father* [God foreknew, God chose], *in sanctification of the Spirit* [the Holy Spirit]." It is through a sanctifying operation that the Holy Spirit brings us to the place of *"obedience"* to the gospel and, through obedience, to the *"sprinkling of the blood of Jesus Christ."* We have gone from the action of the Father in eternity to the sanctifying work of the Spirit in time—drawing, separating, and revealing.

Now, we return to 2 Thessalonians 2:13:

> *But we are bound to give thanks to God always for you, brethren beloved by the Lord, because God from the beginning chose you for salvation* [the end of God's choice is salvation] *through sanctification by the Spirit.*

Paul began his explanation in the above verse with a statement about God's choice. God's foreknowledge is part of the choice, although that is not specifically stated here. Once again, we see that the agent who brings us to salvation is the Holy Spirit, by His sanctifying operation. He brings us to the place where we accept the truth of the gospel, obey it, and enter into salvation. An important factor to understand, therefore, is that the Holy Spirit's work begins before we believe the gospel and consciously receive salvation.

> **The agent who brings us to salvation is the Holy Spirit, by His sanctifying operation.**

God's Work in the Lives of Paul and Jeremiah

It will be instructive for us to look at two remarkable statements about two great men of the Bible, Paul and Jeremiah. The first is in Galatians 1:15, where Paul said this about himself:

> *But when it pleased God, who separated me from my mother's womb and called me through His grace....*

Paul said he was *"separated"* from his mother's womb. From the very moment of Paul's birth, God began to set him aside for His special purposes. Yet, for some years, Paul was actually the chief persecutor of the church. During that time, Paul was not conscious of salvation, for he had not acknowledged Jesus Christ. Actually, he openly opposed the gospel. And yet, all that time, God the Holy Spirit was moving in his life to separate him and to bring him to the place where God's intended destiny could be fulfilled.

The prophet Jeremiah made a similar statement about himself in Jeremiah 1:4–5:

> *Then the word of the LORD came to me, saying: "Before I formed you in the womb I knew you; before you were born I sanctified you; I ordained you a prophet to the nations."*

Notice that Jeremiah's destiny was settled when he was still in his mother's womb. God told Jeremiah that before he was formed in the womb, He knew him. And before Jeremiah was born, God sanctified him—set him apart—for the purpose He had for his life: to be *"a prophet to the nations."* In regard to that purpose, God said, *"I ordained you."*

God's purposes for Jeremiah began to be worked out while he was still in his mother's womb. Yet, at the time when God spoke to him, Jeremiah essentially said, "Lord, don't call me. I can't be a prophet. I'm too young." (See verse 6.) Jeremiah was not conscious of the divine destiny that had begun to work in his life even before his birth. In fact, he was at first unwilling to accept that divine destiny.

We see in the lives of Paul and Jeremiah alike that the sanctifying work of the Holy Spirit begins before we come to a conscious awareness of salvation, or to any kind of acceptance by our wills of God's purpose and program for our lives.

God's Intervention in Our Conscious Experience

Having recognized God's operation, first in eternity and then in time, we come now to the point in time when God actually intervenes in our conscious experience, so that our destiny brings us to hear the preaching of the cross. We see this intervention as we look briefly again at 2 Thessalonians 2. Paul wrote,

> *God from the beginning chose you for salvation through sanctification of the Spirit and belief in the truth, to which He called you by our gospel.*   (verses 13–14)

The moment of being called is when God's destiny is revealed to us through the preaching of His Word, when we are brought to the place where we must respond and make a personal commitment to the demand of God upon our lives.

We see the same truth in the book of Romans:

> *For whom He foreknew, He also predestined to be conformed to the image of His Son, that He* [Jesus] *might be the firstborn among many brethren* [which includes all believers]. *Moreover whom He predestined, these He also called.*   (Romans 8:29–30)

This passage describes God's divine intervention in time—in our personal, conscious experience. We physically hear the gospel being proclaimed, and, as the Word of God is preached, we spiritually hear the call of almighty God. This is the watershed of human experience.

I never make that last statement without thinking of when I was in Denver, Colorado, many years ago. Some people took me there on a trip to the eastern slope of the Rocky Mountains, where they pointed a little farther to the west and said, "Just over there is the watershed of the North American continent." At that moment, a vivid picture of what the word *watershed* meant came into my mind.

I thought about two drops of rain or two flakes of snow descending from heaven and landing right along this watershed. I could see in my mind one on the western slope and the other

> **There is a critical moment of decision when we have to say yes or no to the call of God and to the claims of Jesus Christ.**

on the eastern slope, separated maybe by two inches in the place where they fell. Yet their destinies would be totally different. The one that fell on the western slope would end up in the Pacific Ocean, while the one that fell on the eastern slope would end up, possibly, in the Gulf of Mexico or the Atlantic Ocean. There would be a difference of thousands of miles in their ultimate destinations. Yet the initial difference was maybe just two inches.

That is the watershed—the point of division. And that is what the cross is. It is the watershed of every human life. It is the point of division, the point where our destinies are settled in experience. There is a critical moment of decision when we have to say yes or no to the call of God and to the claims of Jesus Christ.

Paul talked about this watershed moment in 1 Corinthians:

> *For the message of the cross is foolishness to those who are perishing, but to us who are being saved it is the power of God.* (1 Corinthians 1:18)

Please understand that the cross does not change; the message does not change. Yet, it is our response that decides our destinies. If we accept it and submit to it, we are entering into salvation. If we refuse it and reject it, we are perishing.

Again, the division is at the cross, which is the watershed, the most vital moment of decision and destiny in human experience.

Paul expressed this watershed moment in a different way in Philippians 3:12:

> *Not that I have already attained, or am already perfected; but I press on, that I may lay hold of that for which Christ Jesus has also laid hold of* ["*apprehended*" KJV] *me.*

I like that word *"apprehended."* It certainly applies to my personal experience. *Apprehended* suggests to me the great hand of almighty God, reaching down at a given point and a given moment and touching a human life. It is the moment of choice; the moment of destiny; the moment of calling when God's hand stretches down out of heaven, the moment when He apprehends a person for a purpose He planned from eternity but only gradually reveals to that person in time as he or she yields to His call. After such a moment, that life can never be the same again.

Let's summarize what we have examined so far in this chapter and place it into context to make it as clear as possible. First, the Father foreknows, chooses, and predestines. All those actions take place in eternity. Then, the Holy Spirit comes to work out the Father's choice and destiny. Those actions take place in time. It is through the sanctification of the Spirit that God's plans come into force in our lives. I have divided the Holy Spirit's work of sanctification into three actions: drawing, separating, and revealing. This is how I understand sanctification.

In John 6:44, Jesus said,

> *No one can come to Me unless the Father who sent Me draws him.*

The initial move comes from God, not man. No one comes to Jesus Christ by his own initial choice. The initial choice is with God the Father. Jesus confirmed this truth in John 15:16:

You did not choose Me, but I chose you and appointed ["ordained" KJV] you....   (John 15:16)

> **The course of your life could have gone in any given direction if the Holy Spirit had not begun to move upon you.**

Never be deceived about this. The initiative in salvation is with God, not with man. All that man may do is to respond to God's choice when it is revealed to him. So, the Holy Spirit draws. In drawing, He separates. In separating, He brings us to the point of revelation.

The course of your life could have gone in any given direction if the Holy Spirit had not begun to move upon you. But when the Holy Spirit moved upon you, He started to draw you in a different direction from that in which you normally would have gone. As He drew you in that direction, He began to separate you from the course that you would previously have followed. Then, He brought you to a specific point, which was the preaching of the cross—when you heard the gospel proclaimed or you read the gospel in the Word of God.

A New Direction

The Holy Spirit's entrance into our lives can be imperceptible, mostly unrecognized, and often not understood. But He draws us in a new direction. I can remember vividly when this started to happen in my own life. All the pursuits that had been so tremendously exciting and attractive to me lost their appeal. I just could not understand it.

I would go out to dances, which I used to love, and drinking parties, and would promptly fall asleep at midnight. I thought,

I must be getting old before my time. But the Holy Spirit had already begun to separate me. All those pleasures, those entertainments, and those activities began to seem so strange and remote. I thought, *How could I have found pleasure in those things?*

At that point, I knew nothing of salvation. I knew of no alternative lifestyle. I just thought, *Life is losing its real significance. I've lost my taste for pleasure. I don't have the appetites I used to have.*

Then, there came a moment when I was confronted with the preaching of the cross. As far as I was concerned, no one had to tell me; I knew very clearly that I had to make a choice. Also, I knew I had no right to expect that God would give me a second chance. He might have, but one thing I knew with absolute certainty was that if I did not respond at that point, I might never have another opportunity. I thank God that, by the divine intervention of the Holy Spirit, I responded.

Earlier, I wrote about how I first heard the gospel in a Pentecostal assembly, and how, when the appeal was made, I could not understand what they were talking about. I sat there in the silence, just wondering what was going to happen. They said, "Anybody who wants (whatever it was that I could not understand), put up your hand."

Recall that there were two inaudible voices speaking to me. One said, *Now, if you put your hand up in front of all these old ladies as a soldier in uniform, you're going to look very silly.* The other voice said simultaneously in the opposite ear, *If this is something good, why shouldn't you have it?* I was paralyzed, unable to respond to either voice. But, as I sat there in the silence, a miracle took place. The Holy Spirit actually moved my arm up for me. With shock and surprise, I realized that my arm had gone up without my moving it. By the way, that is as far as the Holy Spirit can go. He can give you a little push, but, in the end, you have to make a decision.

Two nights later, I attended another service. I still did not understand much about the gospel, but when they made the appeal, I said to myself, *Well, somebody else did it for me last time.* I could not expect that to happen twice. That time, I put my own arm up. I did not get saved, as I'd already been saved, but I took personal responsibility for that decision.

The Holy Spirit will bring you just as far as He can and just as close as He can. But ultimately, you have to make the personal decision to receive salvation through Jesus Christ.

Crossing the Blood Line

> **When you cross over the blood line, you pass out of Satan's territory and into God's territory.**

So, at the proclamation of the gospel, you make your decision. Your destiny is settled by your response. The cross is what I call the "blood line." When you come to the cross, submit to it, acknowledge Jesus Christ, and bow before Him, then you cross over the blood line. You pass out of Satan's territory into God's territory. You move over into the *"inheritance of the saints in the light"* (Colossians 1:12). Again, the point of division is the cross; the dividing line is the line made by the shed blood of Jesus.

We understand that the sanctifying work of the Holy Spirit is taking place all along. Before you are saved, even before you are conscious of God's plan, He draws you out from the crowd—the multitude of those who will not respond or listen. He separates you. Your life begins to take a different course, and He brings you to the place where He opens your eyes to see Jesus and the cross. Then, you must respond because, after that, there is no more neutrality—you align yourself with either God or Satan.

If you submit to the cross, if you obey the gospel, then you cross over the blood line. Let me just ask you now: Have you taken that step? Have you crossed the blood line? If you haven't, and you wish to do so now, please pray this simple prayer of commitment:

> Lord Jesus Christ, I believe that You are the Son of God and that You are the only way to God. You died on the cross for my sins and You rose again from the dead. I'm sorry now for all my sins. I ask You to forgive me, to cleanse me in Your precious blood. I open my heart to You, Lord Jesus. I invite You in. By simple faith, I receive You now as my Savior, and I confess You as my Lord. Come into my heart. Give me eternal life. Make me a child of God. Thank You, Lord. Amen.

It's wonderful that you have taken this step. Bear in mind that the Holy Spirit's sanctifying work is not yet complete. He goes on sanctifying after salvation, as we shall see.

14

THE BLOOD AND THE WORD

Having seen how God intervenes to direct our lives in eternity and in time, and how the Holy Spirit helps us to come to the blood line, we come now to a closer look at the application of the blood and the continual washing with the water of the Word.

The first Scripture we will examine is 1 Peter 1:1–2, which, by now, you are becoming very familiar with:

> *To the...elect according to the foreknowledge of God the Father, in sanctification* [through the sanctifying work] *of the Spirit, for obedience* [to the gospel. And as a result of obedience, what follows?] *and sprinkling of the blood of Jesus Christ.*

The blood is not applied in our lives until we obey, until we submit, until we yield to the claims of God upon us. But when we obey, the Holy Spirit, who is the administrator of the blood of Jesus, sprinkles us, and we are cleansed, redeemed, and set apart for God.

Entering Our Inheritance

When we cross the blood line, we enter into our inheritance in Jesus Christ. Let's review what Jesus said Paul would do for the Gentiles as he preached the gospel to them:

*...to open their eyes, in order to turn them from dark-
ness to light, and from the power of Satan to God, that
they may receive forgiveness of sins and an inheritance among those who are sanctified by faith in Me.*
(Acts 26:18)

Our sins are forgiven through the blood of Jesus. When
our sins are forgiven through the blood, then we pass over into
the *"inheritance"* of those who are sanctified by faith in Jesus
Christ.

Other Scripture passages track along this line of inheritance, one of which is Ephesians 1:7, 11:

In Him [Christ] *we have redemption through His blood,
the forgiveness of sins, according to the riches of His
grace....In Him also we have obtained an inheritance,
being predestined according to the purpose of Him
who works all things according to the counsel of His
will.*

When we receive forgiveness of sins, we have redemption
and have obtained an inheritance in Christ. We are brought by
the blood of Jesus out of Satan's territory and into the kingdom
of Christ. Colossians brings out this truth:

*Giving thanks unto the Father, which hath made us
meet* [capable] *to be partakers of the inheritance of the
saints in light: who hath delivered us from the power of
darkness, and hath translated [*"transferred"* NASB] *us
into the kingdom of his dear Son.*
(Colossians 1:12–13 KJV)

Here again, the blood of Jesus is the dividing line between
darkness and light, between the power of Satan and the power
of God. Through the blood, God has made us capable *"to be
partakers of the inheritance of the saints in light."*

Total Transfer Through the Blood

There is a "translation" that takes place when the blood of Jesus is applied in our lives. We are carried over totally—spirit, soul, and body—out of Satan's territory and into Christ's territory. The word *translation* indicates a total transfer. There were two men in the Old Testament who were translated: Enoch and Elijah. Each of them was entirely translated—spirit, soul, and body—into heaven without dying. All Elijah left behind was his mantle for his successor, Elisha, to pick up. When Colossians 1:13 (KJV) says we are *"translated,"* it means that our total personality has been moved by divine operation out of Satan's territory and into *"the kingdom of* [God's] *dear Son."*

> **The cross terminates Satan's authority and brings us under the kingdom of Christ, which is a kingdom of love.**

The dividing line between the two territories is the place where the blood is applied. The cross terminates Satan's authority and brings us out of his kingdom of hatred and darkness into the kingdom of Jesus Christ, which is a kingdom of love.

The *New King James Version* says it clearly:

He has delivered us from the power of darkness and conveyed us into the kingdom of the Son of His love, in whom we have redemption through His blood, the forgiveness of sins. (Colossians 1:13–14)

That is a mighty statement, isn't it? We have been delivered *"from the power of darkness and conveyed"*—carried over, transferred, translated—*"into the kingdom of the Son of His love."*

Continual Cleansing by the Word

The application of the blood is a key moment in our transition into the kingdom of God. This truth cannot be overemphasized. However, there is another important factor in our ongoing progress in holiness. After the application of the blood, we come to the continual washing with the water of the Word.

We see this important principle in the book of Ephesians:

Christ...loved the church and gave Himself for her [in redemption on the cross], *that He might* [thereafter] *sanctify and cleanse her with the washing of water by the word....* (Ephesians 5:25–26)

Christ redeemed the church—all believers—by His blood so that He might then sanctify her with the washing of water by His Word—toward His end purpose, which is stated in verse 27:

...that He might present her to Himself a glorious church, not having spot or wrinkle or any such thing, but that she should be holy and without blemish.

As we have seen, the holiness of the church is not achieved merely through the redemption of the blood. It is through redemption by Christ's blood followed by washing and cleansing by the water of the Word.

The Laver: An Old Testament Parallel to the Washing by the Word

This matter of washing and cleansing is beautifully illustrated in the Old Testament by a specific piece of furniture in the tabernacle—the Israelites' place of worship before the temple was built. That item is the laver, which was a vessel used to hold water for cleansing in relation to priestly functions.

In one way or another, everything in the tabernacle represents Jesus Christ, the Christian life, and God's provision for us. That is why so much attention is devoted to the tabernacle in the Old Testament. There are approximately forty chapters that deal with it. An entire listing of the items of furniture in the tabernacle and the relationship of these items to each other, as well as other details, occurs twice in the Old Testament. The tabernacle is therefore extremely important and one of the greatest means of teaching about Christ and the Christian life.

We see this importance, in part, in Exodus 30:

Then the LORD spoke to Moses, saying: "You shall also make a laver of bronze, with its base also of bronze, for washing. You shall put it between the tabernacle of meeting and the altar. And you shall put water in it, for Aaron and his sons shall wash their hands and their feet in water from it. When they go into the tabernacle of meeting, or when they come near the altar to minister, to burn an offering made by fire to the LORD, they shall wash with water, lest they die. So they shall wash their hands and their feet, lest they die. And it shall be a statute forever to them; to him and his descendants throughout their generations."

(verses 17–21)

We need to take note that there was a double provision for the priest: the altar of sacrifice and the laver of clean water. Only through the double provision could the priests achieve the holiness that was necessary to carry out their spiritual duties. The same principle applies to our spiritual lives.

Those approaching the tabernacle approached it through the gateway of the court. The first item that confronted them— that they could not bypass, that stood clearly in their way—was the altar of sacrifice, overlaid with bronze, where the blood of the sacrificed animals was sprinkled. This placement signifies that no one can approach God except on the basis of Christ's death on the cross. No sinner can approach God without a propitiatory sacrifice. And the only sacrifice acceptable to God is the sinner's substitute, Jesus, who shed His blood and forfeited His life on the cross. So, the first great truth inside the tabernacle is depicted by this altar, which speaks of the blood. The blood reconciles the sinner to God and then sets the newly reconciled one apart; it moves him out of Satan's kingdom and into God's territory.

Before the priest could go from the altar to the tabernacle, he had to go by way of the laver of bronze. A close reading of the above Scripture reveals that he was never permitted to pass in either direction without stopping to wash both his hands and his feet in the laver. The laver was an indispensable part of God's provision for the priest.

The laver symbolizes the Word of God, which cleanses and transforms us. As we meditate on and obey the Word of God, we are changed progressively—in character, in attitudes, and in outlook, as well as in our daily conduct and behavior.

> **As we meditate on and obey the Word of God, we are changed in character and in outlook, as well as in our daily conduct.**

God said the priest would die if he ever failed to wash in the laver. We often emphasize how essential the blood is, but if the water was not applied, the penalty was death. I cannot imagine any stronger way of emphasizing the absolute, vital importance of Christians not merely trusting in Jesus' blood for redemption, but also submitting to the Word of God for their continual, progressive cleansing and sanctification.

One aspect of the Old Testament picture of the laver that has become very vivid to me comes from the ordinance for the laver that we looked at earlier.

*Then the LORD spoke to Moses, saying: "You shall also
make a laver of bronze, with its base also of bronze, for
washing."* (Exodus 30:17–18)

My understanding of the metals used in the tabernacle
and, later, in the temple, is that gold represents the nature of
God and holiness, silver represents redemption, and bronze
represents judgment. Note that the altar, the place of judgment,
was made of bronze. Also, both pure gold and beaten gold were
used in the tabernacle. The pure gold is God Himself; the beaten
gold is the church, which has to be shaped into His likeness.
(See Romans 8:29.)

*So they shall wash their hands and their feet, lest they
die. And it shall be a statute forever to them; to him
and his descendants throughout their generations.*
(verse 21)

We see that this bronze laver, which we do not often hear
much about, was an essential and a permanent part of the
priestly ministry for the Israelites. The priest could neither approach the tabernacle from the altar nor come back from the
tabernacle to the altar without washing in the laver. I think that
"the washing of water by the word" mentioned in Ephesians 5:26
is an exact parallel to the role of the laver.

How the Blood and the Water Work Together

To further emphasize these points, let's return to a verse
in 1 John 5:

*This is He who came by water and blood; Jesus Christ;
not only by water, but by water and blood. And it is the
Spirit who bears witness, because the Spirit is truth.*
(verse 6)

These two components—the blood of Jesus' redeeming sacrifice and the water of the regular cleansing and sanctifying of

the Word of God—have to go together. Without the blood, we have no access; we have no life. But without the Word, we are not cleansed; we are not sanctified. Our impurities are not washed away, nor are we fit for the presence of God.

So we have, first, redemption by blood and, second, cleansing and sanctifying by the water of the Word. The total operation produces a church that is holy and acceptable to God. It shows us that redemption by the blood alone is not the ultimate goal. The ultimate goal is redemption first, followed by sanctifying and cleansing by the Word.

> **Without the blood, we have no life. But without the Word, we are not sanctified.**

15

LOOKING IN THE MIRROR

We have seen the importance of the washing and cleansing aspect of the laver in the tabernacle under the old covenant, especially as it foreshadowed the washing by the water of the Word fulfilled under the new covenant. In this chapter, we will focus on another aspect of the laver—its mirrorlike quality, which parallels the role of the Word of God.

Let me begin by explaining another of the laver's interesting qualities, which is mentioned in Exodus 38:8. Generally, we are told very little in the Bible about where the materials came from to make the items of furniture in the tabernacle. But, in the case of the laver, we are told about its material, and I am sure God had a purpose in having it recorded.

> *He* [Bezalel, who made all the furniture for the tabernacle] *made the laver of bronze and its base of bronze, from the bronze mirrors of the serving women who assembled at the door of the tabernacle of meeting.*
> (Exodus 38:8)

In the days of the tabernacle, the Israelites did not have glass mirrors. Their mirrors were made of very highly polished brass or bronze. What this verse tells us is that, in order to make this laver, the women had to sacrifice their mirrors. The idea here is not that a woman should not make herself attractive in her outward appearance. Rather, the overriding thought is a transfer of emphasis from what we look like in the natural mirror to what we look like in the spiritual mirror of God's Word.

God lays the emphasis on the inward beauty of holiness rather than on mere outward, physical beauty, which the Bible says is *"vain"* and will surely pass away. (See Proverbs 31:30 KJV, NKJV.) God is giving us a hint here that it is time for us to put more importance on what we look like inwardly and less importance on what we look like outwardly. We must replace concern for physical appearance with a concern for spiritual experience.

The mirror aspect of the laver gives us a direct connection between the operation of washing by water and the function of the mirror. Let's look at a New Testament verse that conveys this idea. In James, we are told that, among other attributes, the Word of God is like a mirror.

> *For if anyone is a hearer of the word and not a doer,*
> *he is like a man observing his natural face in a mirror;*
> *for he observes himself, goes away, and immediately*
> *forgets what kind of man he was.*   (James 1:23–24)

It is possible to look in a mirror, see all sorts of flaws that need adjustment—your hair is untidy, your face is dirty, your tie is crooked, there is a stain on your suit—and then walk away, forgetting the flaws you saw and taking no action to remedy them. The result is that you might just as well have not looked in the mirror at all.

James was saying that if you read the Bible or hear the Word preached, and you see your needy spiritual condition but take no corrective action, then you are like a person who looks in the mirror and sees things that need adjustment but does nothing about them. The mirror has done that person no ultimate good whatsoever.

On the positive side, James went on to say,

> *But he who looks into the perfect law of liberty and*
> *continues in it* [after he has read the Bible or heard the preaching, he acts on it and maintains obedience],

*and is not a forgetful hearer but a doer of the work,
this one will be blessed in what he does.* (James 1:25)

Our Inward Spiritual Condition

The Word of God, therefore, is like a mirror that is held up
before us and shows us our inward spiritual condition.

We Have a Responsibility to Act on What We See

At deliverance services, I tell the people, "Don't expect me
to walk up to you, stick my finger between your eyes, and say,
'You have a demon, and you need to get rid of it.'" I don't do that.
Instead, I hold up the mirror of the Word so that they can look
in it and can then act on what they see. It is their decision and
their responsibility—not mine.

Actually, this is true of all preaching, teaching, and ministering. We preachers can hold up the mirror, but you to whom
we preach are responsible to act on what you see. And, if you
see and do not act, it does you no good. In fact, it brings you
condemnation instead of blessing.

We have seen from the Scriptures we have studied that
the mirror and the laver were both made of the same metal,
which was bronze. Earlier, I talked about three basic metals
and their spiritual significance in Scripture. Let's review those
statements to make them clear: gold stands for the divine nature and for holiness, silver stands for redemption, and bronze
stands for judgment.

You will find these principles at work all through the
Scriptures. For example, on the Isle of Patmos, John the
Revelator saw Jesus in His glory, and *"His feet were like
burnished bronze, when it has been caused to glow in a fur-
nace"* (Revelation 1:15 NASB). That is a picture of Christ coming to judge the wicked—to trample them under His feet in
judgment.

We Need to Judge Ourselves

When we look in the mirror of God's Word and see our true condition, God expects us to judge ourselves by what we see. This truth is clearly expressed in a statement by the apostle Paul, who was inspired by the Holy Spirit to show us that this responsibility is ours:

> For if we would judge ourselves, we would not be judged. (1 Corinthians 11:31)

The highest level on which to live is the level on which we judge ourselves (assess our behavior or attitude) by what we see in the Word. Verse 32 completes the thought:

> But when we are judged [by God as believers], we are chastened [punished, disciplined] by the Lord, that we may not be condemned with the world.

Again, the highest level in the Christian life is not that God should have to continue punishing us, but that, when we look in the mirror of the Word and see something wrong in our lives, we act to change it without having to be punished.

If we do not act upon it, God will then apply His discipline and start chastening us. His object in doing so is to prevent us from going the way of the world into condemnation. But if we resist God's chastening and go the way of the world, then we come into the same judgment that comes to the world. "If we say that we have no sin, we deceive ourselves, and the truth is not in us" (1 John 1:8).

> **When we look in the mirror of the Word and see something wrong in our lives, we act to change it.**

On the other hand, we can look in the mirror of God's Word and see clearly revealed there something wrong in our lives—some fault, some error, some wrong emphasis, some bad attitude. Then we take the step of judging ourselves. We say, "That's wrong. I shouldn't be doing it. I renounce it. Lord, I repent. Please deliver me from it." If we take that action, God will not have to chasten us. *"If we confess our sins, He is faithful and just to forgive us our sins and to cleanse us from all unrighteousness"* (1 John 1:9).

I find that many Christians run into all sorts of experiences of chastening that they easily could have avoided if they had only acted upon what God showed them in the mirror of His Word. Many of your troubles are not persecution for righteousness' sake. (Don't deceive yourself.) They are the results of your own stubbornness, of going your own way and refusing to change, in spite of the fact that God showed you your condition by His Word. So, God said, "All right, I'll have to start disciplining you, because you wouldn't avail yourself of what the mirror showed you."

I do not believe that choosing to serve Jesus Christ is a terribly hard option. Personally, it grieves me when I hear preachers indicating that if you decide to serve Christ, everything will go wrong. That isn't true. I tell you plainly that, when you serve Christ, there may be persecution and problems in your Christian life. But if you decide not to serve Christ, it will be far worse. Be sure of that.

Certainly, there are persecutions and oppositions in the Christian life. But so much of what we run into is not persecution or opposition. It is God's chastening for our pigheadedness, because we saw what He was trying to show us in the Word but refused to act on it.

The Beauty of the Mirror

On the other side of the ledger, the beautiful thing about this mirror is that it shows you more than just how bad you look. When you have acted on what God requires of you, and you look again in the mirror, do you know what you see? You see Jesus Christ, and you see what you can be in God's sight through Christ.

Another reference to this wonderful mirror is one that talks about the contrast to the Israelites who were under the law of Moses. After Moses had met with God, he found it necessary to veil his face so that the people wouldn't see God's glory fading from it, until he met with God again. (See 2 Corinthians 3:11–16; Exodus 34:28–35.) There was a certain incompleteness of revelation indicated by the veil. But Paul said for us under the new covenant, the conditions are different:

> *But we all, with unveiled face, beholding as in a mirror the glory of the Lord, are* [continuously] *being transformed into the same image* [the same image that we behold in the mirror] *from glory to glory, just as by the Spirit of the Lord.* (2 Corinthians 3:18)

Here is a tremendous truth for you to grasp: the Spirit of the Lord can work in you for good only while you are in a certain position. What is that position? Looking in the mirror of the Word. If you take your eyes off the mirror of the Word, the Spirit of God cannot work in you. The Spirit works while you are looking in the mirror of the Word to change you into who God wants you to be. As you look in the mirror, you see the glory of Christ, the beauty of holiness. And the Spirit of God changes you into the likeness of what you behold.

> **As you see the glory of Christ, the beauty of holiness, the Spirit of God changes you into the likeness of what you behold.**

That is God's program for transforming you, for sanctifying you experientially, for changing your reactions, your desires, your attitudes, your moods, and your passions. They are changed when you look in the mirror of God's Word and believe what you see. The Holy Spirit changes you *"from glory to glory."*

There is an ever-increasing unveiling and unfolding of the glory of Jesus Christ in the mirror of the Word that is available only to the believer who *continues* looking in the mirror. The problem with so many of us is that, when problems come, we take our eyes off the mirror.

I have always been impressed by the words that are written in the book of Hebrews about Moses:

> *By faith he forsook Egypt, not fearing the wrath of the king; for he endured as seeing Him who is invisible.*
> (Hebrews 11:27)

That is beautiful. How can you see the invisible? Not with the natural eye, not in situations or circumstances, but in the mirror. The mirror shows you the invisible—the eternal.

Looking Past Affliction to the Unseen World

Paul talked about the principle of looking into the eternal and seeing the invisible in 2 Corinthians 4:17–18. He began with these words: *"For our light affliction"* (verse 17). The phrase *"light affliction"* makes me wonder why some people today complain about their lives. Paul was beaten five times, stoned once, and shipwrecked twice. Read the list of what he went through, found in 2 Corinthians 11:23–28, and then hear Paul refer to *"our light affliction."*

Some people try to tell you that Paul was a kind of invalid. They say that he had a sickness of the eyes and that he hobbled around. All I can say is, if Paul was an invalid, give us more invalids like him in the church! Any man who could put up with what Paul went through isn't much of an invalid. But, after listing all these dire experiences, Paul said,

For our light affliction, which is but for a moment, is working for us a far more exceeding and eternal weight of glory, while we do not look at the things which are seen, but at the things which are not seen. For the things which are seen are temporary [transient, impermanent], *but the things which are not seen are eternal* [they last forever].   (2 Corinthians 4:17–18)

Where are we to *"look"*? At the eternal, invisible things in the mirror of God's Word. And, while we look, our *"light afflictions"* are producing the divine purpose. However, if we take our eyes off the mirror, then the Holy Spirit will stop operating until we get our eyes back on the mirror of the Word again.

Paul expressed the goal of this process of divine intervention by the Holy Spirit. Speaking about his ministry to the Gentiles, he said,

That I might be a minister of Jesus Christ to the Gentiles, ministering the gospel of God, that the offering [to God] *of the Gentiles might be acceptable* [to Him], *sanctified by the Holy Spirit.*   (Romans 15:16)

In the original Greek, the tense used here is actually the perfect tense: "[having been] *sanctified by the Holy Spirit."* What Paul described is the purpose of the process by which the Holy Spirit sanctifies us—a process that began before we even knew God. He drew us, separated us, revealed the cross to us, brought us to the blood line, carried us over, and continuously sanctifies us while we are looking in the mirror and being washed with the water of the Word.

The ultimate purpose of all that had taken place would be that the offering up of the Gentiles (the non-Jewish believers in Jesus Christ) might be acceptable to God, having been fully, completely, perfectly sanctified by the Holy Spirit. And that same purpose applies to us.

16

FAITH AND WORKS—
OUR RESPONSE

We have examined all that God has provided for us, including the work of Jesus and the Holy Spirit, in order that we may answer His call to be holy. In this chapter, we will discuss in greater detail our response to God's intervention in our lives— that is, our faith and our works.

Indispensable Faith

First of all, let's talk about our faith. There is a point where God cannot move beyond our faith. At the beginning of the process by which He draws us to Himself, God moves without our exercising active faith. But the culmination of His purposes depends upon our responding in faith. There is a moment when faith becomes indispensable if God's purposes are to be fulfilled in our lives.

Connecting to what we discussed in the previous chapter, by faith, we accept what we see in the mirror of God's Word. We look in the mirror, we repent of our sins, we change our ways, we submit ourselves to divine discipline, *"we walk in the light as He is in the light"* (1 John 1:7), and we *"walk in the truth"* (3 John 1:3) of the Word of God. When we do these things, as I mentioned previously, we are in a position to accept by faith the beautiful truths about ourselves that we find in God's Word. Bear in mind, we are not outside of Christ, nor outside of the grace of God. We are believers who have taken our places in Christ and are in right standing with God.

Let's now take a closer look at a series of very encouraging statements. Each of these statements applies to all believers, but must also be accepted by you as an individual believer, through faith, if they are to be effective in your life. (Please note that the following is not an exhaustive list of statements about our experience in Christ.)

"Accepted in the Beloved"

Ephesians 1:6 says that God *"has made us accepted in the Beloved." "The Beloved"* is Jesus Christ. Is it so important for you to realize that God *wants* you.

The word *"accepted"* in the above verse really does not do justice to the depth of this truth. The Greek word is *charitoo*, which means "to grace," "endue with special honor," "make accepted," and "be highly favored." The same word is used of the Virgin Mary when the angel Gabriel appeared to her and said, *"Rejoice, highly favored [charitoo] one"* (Luke 1:28). The angel was saying, in other words, "You are graciously accepted; you are the object of divine grace and favor." In Christ, every believer becomes the object of special grace and favor.

God welcomes us. Multitudes of people are walking through life feeling rejected. Their parents have rejected them, their friends have rejected them, society rejects them, and sometimes even the church rejects them. What they must realize is that when they come to God in Christ, they are accepted by Him, not just tolerated. Again, it is vital for you to understand that you are accepted in Christ. Many times, I have led people in a confession like this:

> I thank You, God, that I am accepted in Jesus Christ. God is my Father. Heaven is my home. I am a member of God's family. I belong. I'm not merely tolerated; I am accepted.

No Condemnation

Romans 8:1 gives us another wonderful truth about our experience in Christ:

There is therefore now no condemnation to those who are in Christ Jesus.

> **The past has been dealt with. You are justified by the blood of Jesus.**

You are not condemned. You are not guilty. The past has been dealt with. You are justified by the blood of Jesus. (See Romans 5:9.) You have probably heard this definition of the word *justified*: "Just as if I'd' never sinned." That is what it means to be justified. We have been made righteous with the righteousness of Christ—a righteousness in which even the devil can find no flaw or spot.

Set Apart for God

In addition, Hebrews 13:12 tells us that we are sanctified by the blood of Jesus: *"That He might sanctify the people with His own blood."* That means we are set apart for God through the blood of Jesus.

Continually Cleansed

Then, 1 John 1:7 affirms that we are continually cleansed through the blood of Jesus.

But if we [continue to] walk in the light as He is in the light, we have fellowship with one another, and the blood of Jesus Christ His [God's] Son [continually] cleanses us from all sin.

Alive to God

And Romans 6:11 assures us that we are alive with God's life:

Likewise you also, reckon yourselves to be dead indeed to sin, but alive to God in Christ Jesus our Lord.

All of these statements from God's Word are wonderfully true, but we have to accept them by faith. Having accepted them by faith, we then work them out. This is the point where faith must be translated into action—into deeds.

Positive Actions and Works

As we work out the truth of the statements we have accepted by faith, there are two aspects to the outworking. There is the negative—what we don't do. And there is the positive—what we do. Never let the devil confine you to the negative. You must pass through the negative into the positive.

For example, you must be *"dead...to sin"* (Romans 6:11). But, for heaven's sake, don't stay like that! You also have to be *"alive to God"* (verse 11). Dead to sin and alive to righteousness.

In other words, it is not enough only to stop doing wrong things. That does not make you holy, nor is that the nature of God's holiness. In Matthew 5, Jesus explained the relationship between holiness and what we do:

Let your light so shine before men, that they may see your good works and glorify your Father in heaven.
(verse 16)

"Letting your light shine" means doing good works that people are able to see. It is not just following a set of negative rules. It is a positive, powerful force. In fact, I believe that holiness is the most powerful force at work in our universe. To simply retreat into a negative lifestyle of doing nothing bad and call that "holiness" is self-deception. It is not what God means by holiness at all.

We see this truth clearly in Romans 6. Speaking to people who have reckoned themselves dead to sin and alive to God, Paul said,

> *Therefore do not let sin reign in your mortal body, that you should obey it in its lusts. And do not present ["yield" KJV] your members as instruments of unrighteousness to sin....* (verses 12–13)

> **There comes a moment when you have to say no to the devil and no to sin, and truly mean it.**

That is the negative aspect—don't let sin reign over your body any longer; don't yield the members of your body any longer as instruments for sin to control. I once heard somebody say, "Any person who wants to get to heaven has to learn how to say *no* and mean it." That is the truth. There comes a moment when you have to say no to the devil and no to sin, and truly mean it. I assure you, the devil knows when you say it and mean it, and when you say it without meaning it. The result of each of those responses is totally different. So, again, you have to say no to the devil and no to sin, and you have to mean it. That is the first part.

The second part—the positive part—is that you yield your whole body, by deliberate choice, to God the Holy Spirit, for Him to control.

> *...present yourselves to God as being alive from the dead, and your members as instruments of righteousness to God.* (verse 13)

You deny the devil the members of your body and yield them to God instead. In Colossians, we see a further aspect of this necessity:

> *Therefore put to death* [*"mortify"* KJV] *your members which are on the earth: fornication, uncleanness, passion* [*"inordinate affection"* KJV], *evil desire, and covetousness, which is idolatry.* (Colossians 3:5)

To mortify means "to keep dead." First of all, you reckon these fleshly "members" as dead. Second, you keep them dead. Clearly, every person has certain besetting sins, such as lust, greed, malice, gossip, gluttony, and so on. There are certain areas in your life where you have to keep your besetting sins dead. It does not all happen in one instantaneous experience. It happens by ongoing decisions that the besetting problem will not have dominion over you any longer. It is dead. It is dead. It is dead. In other words, you "mortify" it—you keep it dead.

But, of course, it is not enough merely to keep it dead. Again, there has to be a corresponding positive operation, and we find this positive aspect in 1 John 3:3:

> *And everyone who has this hope in Him purifies himself, just as He* [Christ] *is pure.*

In your pursuit of holiness, it is not sufficient to mortify your body. You must also purify your body, and the Scriptures say you do this by obeying the Word of God. This fact is clear from 1 Peter 1:22:

> *Since you have purified your souls in obeying the truth through the Spirit....*

The way we purify our members is by obeying the teaching of God's Word regarding those members. We mortify them, we keep them dead to sin, we purify them, and we also make them increasingly pure and holy.

In Our Relationships

We exercise the negative and the positive aspects of holy living as well in our relationships with other people. The negative action is that we must separate ourselves from the ungodly, the impure, and the unclean. The positive action is that we must associate with the godly, the pure, and the righteous.

This truth is stated in 2 Timothy:

> *But in a great house there are not only vessels of gold and silver, but also of wood and clay, some for honor and some for dishonor.* (verse 20)

The *"great house"* that Paul was writing about is the church. He asserted that in the church there are many different kinds of people, whom he called "vessels." Some are pure; some are not pure. Some are vessels for honor; some are vessels for dishonor.

This is true in our experience today. Wherever we go, we find there are true believers who are leading holy lives. There are also hypocrites, there are false believers, and there are others in a backslidden state who have turned away from God. These people are not leading clean, pure, and holy lives. So, Paul said there are vessels for honor, or vessels that are pure, and there are vessels for dishonor, or vessels that are unclean. Paul's advice to us follows in verse 21:

> *Therefore if anyone cleanses himself from the latter* [the unclean vessels—notice that cleansing is necessary not just for sin but also for wrong associations], *he will be a vessel for honor, sanctified and useful for the Master, prepared for every good work.*

Clearly, there is a time when you must disassociate yourself from those who are not walking in the light, not walking in the truth, not walking in the Spirit and who may even be a negative influence on you. Even though they may be members of a church and may profess faith, they are not vessels for honor but vessels for dishonor. The Scriptures say we must separate ourselves from them. In the same context, the passage continues,

> *Flee also youthful lusts; but pursue righteousness, faith, love, peace with those who call on the Lord out of a pure heart.* (2 Timothy 2:22)

It begins with the negative side—the action of fleeing youthful lusts—and continues with the positive side—the pursuit of good things, such as righteousness, faith, love, and peace. You must pursue these good things in the right company: *"with those who call on the Lord out of a pure heart."* Here, we have the practical outworking of holiness very simply expressed. In every case, there is a negative step followed by a positive step. We must never rest content with simply fulfilling the negative part.

> **The positive aspect of holiness is the pursuit of good things, such as righteousness, faith, love, and peace.**

Let's do a quick review of what we have covered so far in this section:

1. On the negative side, we deny the members of our bodies to sin and to the devil. We say, "No, you can't have me any longer. I won't obey you." Then, on the positive side, we yield to the Holy Spirit. We say to Him, "My members are now at Your disposal; they are instruments of righteousness for You to control."

2. On the negative side, we mortify—we keep dead—those unclean practices that are associated with

the way we lived in the past. On the positive side, we purify ourselves and our members by obeying the Word of God continually.

3. On the negative side, we separate ourselves from people who are "vessels" for dishonor—the impure, the unclean, those who are not walking in the way of holiness. On the positive side, by deliberate choice, we associate with those who are walking in the way of holiness, righteousness, and truth.

This is all part of the outworking of our sanctification.

The Promise Ladder

As we close this chapter, I want to cover three passages that will provide a helpful illustration for us in regard to holiness.

We will begin by returning to a verse in 2 Corinthians:

Therefore, having these promises, beloved, let us cleanse ourselves from all filthiness of the flesh and spirit, perfecting holiness in the fear of God.

(2 Corinthians 7:1)

This verse focuses on the process of cleansing ourselves on the basis of the promises of God's Word. The provision, as I pointed out earlier in this book, is in the promises. As we act upon the promises, we cleanse ourselves from *"all filthiness of the flesh and spirit."*

The next two passages—one from the Old Testament and the other from the New—give us a very beautiful picture. The first is from Genesis 28, which describes the ladder Jacob saw in a dream. This ladder reached to heaven and had God's angels upon it. Jacob experienced this dream at the time when he had to flee from his home. At this point, he was a wanderer because he had been a cheat and a crook. As a result, he was empty-handed. By his own testimony, he had nothing in his hand but a staff that he walked with.

In that condition, Jacob came to a certain place where he was to spend the night. Darkness descended upon him, and he had nowhere to rest, so he lay in the open field with a stone for a pillow. That night, in his emptiness, in his desolation and his desperation, God spoke to him and gave him several promises. Let me tell you that when you come to the end of yourself, that is when God speaks to you. The Lord opened Jacob's eyes in a dream to see this ladder that stretched from earth to heaven, with the angels of God ascending and descending upon it.

With this picture firmly in mind, let's look briefly at one final passage:

> *His divine power has given to us all things that pertain to life and godliness, through the knowledge of Him who called us by glory and virtue, by which have been given to us exceedingly great and precious promises, that through these you may be partakers of the divine nature, having escaped the corruption that is in the world through lust.* (2 Peter 1:3–4)

Putting these two images together, we first have the picture of the ladder that stretches from earth to heaven—symbolically, from the world's corruption to God's holy nature. Second, we have the rungs on that ladder, each of which might be seen as representing a promise from God's Word. Paul wrote in 2 Corinthians 7:1, *"Therefore, having these promises,...let us cleanse ourselves."* In other words, let us climb the ladder, step by step by step. Every time you claim a promise of God,

> **The way to God's holy nature is through standing on His promises.**

you are lifting your foot one rung higher up the ladder toward Him and His holy nature.

Jacob's ladder from earth to heaven is the Word of God and the promises of God. The way up is by standing on the promises of God and claiming them one by one, in progression. As you claim the promises, apply them, and work them out in your life, you escape the world's corruption and become a partaker of the divine nature.

This is how we work out the sanctification that we receive first by faith.

17

PRACTICAL STEPS TOWARD HOLINESS

So far in this book, we have established that God is holy and therefore requires holiness in His people. As impossible as it may seem to achieve holiness, we have learned the good news—God has made provision for our holiness. And that provision comes to us in seven aspects: Jesus Christ, the cross, the Holy Spirit, the blood of Jesus, the Word of God, our faith, and our works (or the actions we take to express our faith).

We have also seen how God's provision works out in our lives in practical ways. His actions on our behalf begin in eternity and are then translated into time. In eternity, God the Father foreknows, chooses, and predestines us. Then, in time, the Holy Spirit begins and continues the work of sanctifying. I suggested that we may split up this work of sanctifying into three actions: drawing, separating, and revealing.

The Holy Spirit begins to draw us, to separate us out from others, and then He brings us to the place where He can reveal to us the truth of Christ and the cross. It is the Holy Spirit who brings us to the blood line. As we cross the blood line under His leading, we move out of Satan's territory into God's territory. Then, of course, the sanctifying work of the Holy Spirit continues from then on.

Jesus: Our Perfect Example of Sanctification

Let's now examine the further practical application of this teaching on holiness by looking at the example of Jesus. This section could just as easily be called "How to Sanctify Yourself." We will cover what you can do practically in response to what God has done and in response to what He has made available to you.

In sanctification, as in every other aspect of the Christian life, Jesus is our perfect Example and Pattern. You may not be aware that Jesus Himself was sanctified. Yet we find a statement to this effect in John 10, where Jesus was discussing with the Jews His claim to be the Son of God. They had disputed and rejected His claim, but He substantiated it using Old Testament Scriptures, which He applied to Himself.

Chosen, Sanctified, and Sent

We won't take time here to delve into the whole scriptural background of Jesus' quotation below, which is from Psalm 82:6 in the Old Testament. Instead, we will just start with the statement He made in the gospel of John that quotes that verse from Psalms:

> *Jesus answered them, "Is it not written in your law, 'I said, "You are gods"'? If He* [God] *called them* [those appointed as judges over the people] *gods, to whom the word of God came (and the Scripture cannot be broken), do you say of Him whom the Father sanctified and sent into the world, "You are blaspheming," because I said, "I am the Son of God"?*
>
> (John 10:34–36)

The Father sanctified the Son, Jesus, and sent Him into the world. This means that the Father chose Jesus in eternity for a specific task that no one else in heaven or on earth could fulfill. Having chosen Jesus, He sanctified Him—He set Him apart for that task. Then, having sanctified Jesus, the Father sent Him at a given moment into the stream of human history to fulfill the task. Jesus was the perfect Pattern: the Father chose Him, the Father sanctified Him, and the Father sent Him.

Let's look next at John 17, where Jesus was praying for His disciples. The theme of verses 16 through 19 is sanctification.

They are not of the world, just as I am not of the world. Sanctify them by Your truth. Your word is truth. As You sent Me into the world, I also have sent them into the world. And for their sakes I sanctify Myself, that they also may be sanctified by the truth. (John 17:16–19)

Please notice Jesus' statement in verse 19: *"I sanctify Myself."* The Father, in eternity, had sanctified Jesus and sent Him to fulfill a special task. But sanctification is not complete until the person who is being sanctified responds to the will of God by his own sanctification. The sanctification of Jesus, therefore, was not complete until He said to the Father, in effect, "Acknowledging what Your choice is, recognizing the task that You have given Me, I now sanctify Myself. I set Myself apart for the fulfillment of the task for which You have sanctified Me and sent Me into the world."

Reviewing these truths, we see that the process of sanctification begins with the Father in eternity. Next, Jesus sanctified Himself to the Father and then to the task to which the Father had sent Him. Through Jesus' actions, we see these principles: as we are sanctified, we respond first to God the Father, the One who sanctifies us,

> **We respond first to God the Father, and we respond second to the task to which we have been appointed.**

and we respond second to the task to which we have been appointed, the task that God has chosen us to accomplish.

I emphasize this point because we need to see that sanctification without a task can often end up as a meaningless religious activity or formula. Sanctification implies two things: a relationship with God and an attitude toward a task. Without the task, the sanctification is not complete.

Jesus' Attitude Toward the Father

We can understand a great deal about sanctification by observing how Jesus related to His Father. Let's look at some Scriptures that describe Jesus' attitudes toward the Father, toward the Father's will, and toward the task the Father had given to Him.

We will look first at Psalm 40:7–8. Please note that these same words are applied to the Lord Jesus Christ by the author of Hebrews. (See Hebrews 10:7.) However, I prefer to take them from the book of Psalms because they are more complete there than in the reference in Hebrews. In Psalm 40, we read,

> *Then I* [the Son] *said, "Behold, I come; in the scroll of the book it is written of me* [in God's eternal purposes and program, there is a part written for me to play]. *I delight to do Your will, O my God, and Your law is within my heart."*   (verses 7–8)

This is the response of the Son to the Father. Discovering the Father's will in the *"book,"* He said, *"In the scroll of the book it is written of me. I delight to do Your will."*

What makes this truth so wonderful to us is that the same book Jesus referred to has something written for each of us. Just as it has something written for Jesus, it has something written for you and me. Our task is to find out what is written for our lives *"in the scroll of the book."*

In the scroll of the book it is written of me [recognizing the purpose of God, I then respond], *I delight to do Your will, O my God, and Your law is within my heart.*

Next, we will consider three passages from the gospel of John that express the relationship of Jesus to the Father as He fulfilled the Father's task. In John 6, Jesus said,

For I have come down from heaven, not to do My own will, but the will of Him who sent Me. (verse 38)

Jesus came specifically to do the will of God, which was revealed in His eternal purposes. When Jesus discovered and discerned the will of God written in the scroll of the book, He said, in essence, "Behold, I have come to do Your will." And He said to the people who were around Him, *"I have come down from heaven, not to do My own will, but the will of Him who sent Me."*

In our next passage, Jesus made this well-known statement to Philip:

Have I been with you so long, and yet you have not known Me, Philip? He who has seen Me has seen the Father; so how can you say, "Show us the Father"? (John 14:9)

By coming to do the Father's will and by doing what God purposed, Jesus revealed the Father. In other words, the way in which He made known the invisible Father to the world was by doing the Father's will—by fulfilling the tasks the Father had appointed for Him.

Our third passage records what Jesus prayed in relation to the task given to Him by the Father:

I have glorified You on the earth. I have finished the work which You have given Me to do. (John 17:4)

In completing the work assigned to Him by the Father, Jesus glorified the Father.

This is the pattern: the Father chose Jesus, sanctified Him, and sent Him to fulfill a task. Jesus discovered the will of God written in the scroll of the book and said, *"Behold, I come...to do Your will"* (Psalm 40:7–8). He testified, *"I have come down from heaven, not to do My own will, but the will of Him who sent Me"* (John 6:38). In doing the Father's will, He was able to say, in effect, "If you have seen Me doing the Father's will, you have seen the Father." (See John 14:9.) And, in fulfilling the task, Jesus said, "I have glorified the Father." (See John 17:4.)

So, Jesus achieved these results: (1) He revealed the Father, and (2) He glorified the Father. We recognize, then, the ultimate purposes of sanctification: to reveal and glorify the One who sanctifies.

Parallel Processes

Now that we have observed this pattern in the relationship of the Father to the Son, and the Son's response to the Father, we will next unfold it in the relationship of Jesus to His disciples. Looking again at John 17, we see that Jesus prayed,

> *Sanctify them by Your truth. Your word is truth. As You sent Me into the world, I also have sent them into the world. And for their sakes I sanctify Myself, that they also may be sanctified by the truth.*   (verses 17–19)

Please notice that the theme all the way through this passage is sanctification. In verse 18, Jesus said to the Father, in essence, "Just as You sent Me into the world, even so, in exactly the same way, I have sent the disciples into the world. And, through fulfilling My will, the disciples will be sanctified as I was sanctified in fulfilling the Father's will." The pattern of Jesus' relationship with the disciples is a perfect pattern of the Father's relationship with Jesus.

Then, if we look carefully at John 20:21, we find the following statement of Jesus. This time, He was not speaking to the Father but directly to the disciples.

Peace to you! As the Father has sent Me, I also send you.

The relationship is exactly parallel. The Father chose, sanctified, and sent Jesus for a specific task that no one else could fulfill. Here in John 20, Jesus emulated that pattern with the disciples, saying to them, in effect, "I have chosen you, I sanctify you, and I send you to fulfill a specific task that no one else can fulfill."

We must remember that sanctification is based on commitment first to God, not to the task. Without the task, sanctification ends up as just a meaningless ritual or an empty doctrine. But without commitment to God, the task becomes an empty work.

Sanctified for a Task

We will now look at a Scripture that will require you to pay close attention to see its application in your life. The verse is Hebrews 2:11:

For both He who sanctifies and those who are being sanctified are all of one, for which reason He is not ashamed to call them brethren.

There are actually three people or groups referred to in the above verse: (1) the One who sanctifies, (2) those who are being sanctified, and (3) the One from whom they all come. Take a moment to figure out who is referred to in each case. Who is the One referred to as *"He who sanctifies"*? (Be careful before you answer.) It would be either the Father or Jesus, wouldn't it? The correct answer is Jesus. Jesus is the One who sanctifies the disciples. Who are *"those who are being sanctified"*? The correct answer is the disciples.

I was giving this teaching years ago in Pittsburgh, Pennsylvania, at a large Presbyterian church. Sitting right in front of me, not in a pew but on the floor, were two little African-American boys. The older of the two could not have been more than twelve years old. I put this question to the audience exactly as I have written it in this section, asking, "Who are those who are sanctified?" Before the question was even out of my mouth, the younger of the two boys popped up and shouted, "The disciples!" I nearly fell over backward at how far ahead he was of the rest of the congregation. He was an unusually perceptive child.

We have one Person left to identify—the one of whom it says they *"are all of one."* Who is that One? The Father, of course. From the Father come *"He who sanctifies"* and *"those who are being sanctified"* by Him. The Father sanctifies the Son; the Son sanctifies the disciples. All proceed from One, who is the Father.

But remember that the sanctification of Jesus was not complete until He had responded to the Father's will and said, "I sanctify Myself. Father, You set Me apart, and now I set Myself apart to the task that You have revealed to Me." In the same way, the sanctification of the disciple is not complete until he, in turn, says, "Jesus, You chose me, You sanctified me, and now I sanctify myself to You and to the task You have for me to do."

To me, the pattern we have just described makes sense of sanctification. Honestly, I have plowed through many years of trying to make sense out of this doctrine of sanctification. All I could come up with, in most cases, was a set of rules: "Do not do this, do not do that, do not do the other. Don't drink, don't smoke, don't dance, don't swear."

I used to tell people when I preached in Copenhagen, "There's a statue in the middle of your city that doesn't drink, doesn't dance, doesn't smoke, doesn't swear. But it isn't a

Christian. If that's all that being a Christian is, just go plant a tree that also doesn't drink, doesn't dance, doesn't smoke, doesn't swear, doesn't go to movies, doesn't wear lipstick or do anything else you could consider wrong, and call it a Christian." As I said, I have had to plow through this matter for myself to arrive at a plain, clear understanding of what sanctification is. And, by the grace of God, I believe I have found it. It is very simple. The Father chose, sanctified, and sent Jesus for a task. Jesus responded by saying, "Father, I've sanctified Myself. Now I'm going to fulfill the task." And He fulfilled it on the cross.

Jesus chooses, sanctifies, and sends the disciples for a task. But each disciple has to respond to Jesus as He responded to the Father. The disciple has to turn to Jesus and say, "Jesus, I acknowledge You've chosen me. I acknowledge You've sanctified me. And now, I sanctify myself for the task to which You've sent me."

The Goal of Sanctification

It is very important for us to understand this pattern in the context of the ultimate purpose for sanctification. We see clearly that in fulfilling the task, the disciple accomplishes for Jesus what Jesus accomplished for the Father. What did Jesus do for the Father? He revealed and glorified Him.

> **The end purpose of our sanctification is to reveal and glorify Jesus.**

This principle applies directly to you, as a disciple. When you discover your task, you set yourself apart, first to Jesus and second to the task. Then, as you do the will of Jesus and fulfill the task, you accomplish these two results: you reveal and glorify Jesus. What, then, is the end purpose of our sanctification? It is to reveal and glorify Jesus.

Many times, God essentially said about His people under the old covenant, "The heathen will know that I am God when I am sanctified in you, My people." (See, for example, Ezekiel 36:23.)

The purpose of sanctification is not to make us different from other people. It is not to make us "holier." It is not to live by a set of negative rules. It is to reveal and glorify Jesus Christ, the One who sanctifies. But that result demands a response from the one who is sanctified, just as Jesus had to respond to the Father, who sanctified Him.

Let's look again at Hebrews 2:11. I trust that it will be much clearer to you now than the first time we discussed it:

> *For both He who sanctifies* [Jesus] *and those who are being sanctified* [Jesus' disciples, or followers] *are all of one* [the Father], *for which reason He is not ashamed to call them brethren.*

Naturally, Jesus is not ashamed to call them brethren, because, in fulfilling His will in sanctification, they show forth His nature. They take on the family likeness. They become like Him—not just in theory, not just by doctrine, but in nature. Experientially, they have proved themselves to be the children of God, demonstrating the nature of the Father and His family.

18

THE BEAUTIFUL SECRET

In this chapter, we will move further into the details of how we can respond to God's choice of us for His purposes.

> *You did not choose Me, but I chose you and appointed* *["ordained"* KJV] *you that you should go and bear fruit, and that your fruit should remain....* (John 15:16)

The choice spoken of here does not initiate with the disciples. The choice initiates with the Lord Jesus Christ. He chooses us. He ordains us so that we will go to fulfill the tasks He has given to us. And in carrying out the tasks, we bring forth lasting spiritual fruit.

As we are moving in fulfillment of His divine purpose, the rest of this Scripture is realized:

> *...that whatever you ask the Father in My name He may give you.* (verse 16)

When you move in the will of God, all frustrations, all hindrances, all frictions disappear. Walking in perfect harmony with the will of God, you accomplish His purposes, and your prayers offered for the fulfillment of His purposes are answered. This is the secret of answered prayer. It is perfect harmony with the will of God.

This was also the secret of the earthly life of Jesus. He was never late. He was never early. He was never hurried. He was never anxious. He was never at a loss. He never lacked anything. Everything He and His disciples needed was always available. Why? Because He moved in absolute harmony with the will of the Father.

Moving in God's Purposes

As you and I learn our part in God's purposes and move in harmony with those tasks to their fulfillment, then, my friend, we begin to see the outworking of Romans 8:28:

> *And we know that all things work together for good to those who love God* [that's not the end of the verse], *to those who are the called* [that's not the end of the verse] *according to His purpose.*

> **The real working together for good of everything in your life comes when you are in harmony with the will of God.**

It is when you are moving in the purposes of God that everything works together for good. It is when you are moving in the purposes of God that whatever you ask the Father in the name of Jesus is done. But the secret of this entire matter is to find the task of God and fulfill it.

You cannot claim the promise of Romans 8:28 when you are not in harmony with the will of God. When you are not moving according to His purposes, there are many things that will not work together for good to you in the best sense. They may be corrections, they may be discipline, they may be warnings, they may be God's means to bring you into line with His will. But the real working together for good of everything in your life comes only when you are in perfect harmony with the will of God. Then, when God has chosen you and sent you, and you move forward in response to Him, you bring forth fruit—fruit that remains.

There are many people in Christian service bringing forth fruit that does not remain, because it was not the fruit God asked them to bring forth. They did not go in obedience to His will. They were "busy beavers," working on their own projects, trying to do their own thing, "volunteering" for God.

But Jesus did not treat His disciples that way. He said, "You didn't choose Me. I chose you." Anything you do outside the choice of God is just wood, hay, and straw that will be burned up on the day of judgment. (See 1 Corinthians 3:11–13.)

"Busy-Beaver" Faith versus Real Faith

I have concluded that the biggest hindrance to real faith is this busy-beaver faith. You may say, for example, "I'm trying to accomplish things, Lord. Do You see how hard I'm praying? I'm determined that this man will be healed." As long as you put all that carnal effort and self-will into your faith, real faith will be a stranger to you.

Over the years, I have heard many empty utterances about praying in faith and agreeing in faith, such as "Let's agree, and it'll be done!" We know perfectly well that, many times, people agree about something, and it isn't done. Why is that? Because there is more to agreeing than just an intellectual decision. For example, let's say we agree that we need to pray for a brother who is in the hospital. There needs to be harmony in that agreement—first, harmony with the will of God; second, harmony between those who pray.

I have learned that when I can stand back and stop being a busy beaver, doing my own thing, it is amazing what God can do. I am convinced that the main reason why the church does not have the faith it should have is that it is so busy doing what God *didn't* ask it to do. Jesus says, "'*You did not choose Me, but I chose you and appointed you that you should go and bear fruit.'* On that basis, your fruit will remain. And on that basis, whatever you ask the Father in My name, He will give you." (See John 15:16.) If that basis is removed, you have no right to those promises.

Created for Good Works

In the book of Ephesians, we see a truth similar to the latter part of Romans 8:28, *"to those who are the called according to His purpose"*:

For we [believers] *are His* [God's] *workmanship, created in Christ Jesus for good works, which God prepared beforehand that we should walk in them.*
(Ephesians 2:10)

We are God's creation. Beloved friend, if you are a Christian, don't criticize yourself. Don't belittle yourself. Don't talk all the time about what you can't do. Don't rehash all your failures. Why shouldn't you talk that way about yourself? Because to do so is to criticize God's workmanship. The Bible says, *"We are His workmanship."*

This thought is expressed in a different way in Romans 9:20: *"Indeed, O man, who are you to reply against God? Will the thing formed say to him who formed it, 'Why have you made me like this?'"* It is not for the clay to tell the potter what to do. The Lord is the Potter; we are the clay. He formed us the way He decided we ought to be because He had a purpose in mind. (See Romans 9:21; Isaiah 64:8.)

"We are His workmanship, created in Christ Jesus for good works, which God prepared beforehand." The words *"prepared beforehand"* mean "before the foundation of the world." God ordained the works—the *"good works"*—that you and I were to walk in. We do not have to decide what we are to be doing. We have to find out what God has chosen for us to do.

I previously worked with a fine group overseas in the mission field. They were great, but I would have to say that I have never attended so many committee meetings in all my life. (In fact, I think I became allergic to committee meetings at that time!) We would get together and say, "What shall we do?" At one point, I told my good missionary brothers, "We stagger out of one crisis just in time to stagger into the next. This cannot be the will of God." What was the problem? We needed to stop trying to decide what we ought to do and find out what God had decided that we should be doing.

Let's stop trying to plan our own lives or our own ministries and missions work. Instead, let's find out what God decided before the foundation of the world we ought to be doing. What a relief it is when you realize you do not have to make the plans! All you have to do is discover the plans that God has already made.

Finding the Beautiful Secret

Let's return briefly to the words of Psalm 40: *"In the scroll of the book it is written of me"* (verse 7). Jesus did not plan His own life and ministry. He found out what God had planned in *"the scroll of the book,"* and then He said, *"Behold, I come...to do Your will"* (verses 7–8).

> **God has something written in the volume of His book just as much for you as He ever had for Jesus.**

This is a beautiful secret, my friend. God has something written in the volume of His book just as much for you as He ever had for Jesus. And you will be truly happy when you have found what is written in the scroll of the book for you and start doing it.

Stop being so busy. Stop being so active. Stop being so "good." Stop being so "spiritual." In other words, come down to earth for a little while. I firmly believe that if something is not practical, then it is not spiritual, either. If it does not work, God isn't in it. Find out what He has written for you in His book and then do what you are called to do in a practical way.

You may wonder, *How can I know the will of God for my life?* That is the theme of our next chapter.

19

A LIVING SACRIFICE

We will now explore an essential aspect of our response to God's choice that enables us to discover His purposes for us and then live accordingly. To do this, we will examine the first six verses of Romans 12. Verse 1 contains the word *"therefore"*: *"I beseech you therefore,..."* Remember that when you find a *"therefore"* in the Bible, it's important to find out what it's "there for," because it links up with something that has gone before it.

To truly understand this *"therefore,"* we need to have an understanding of the progression of the book of Romans. The structure of the book may be summarized in the following way:

- Chapters 1–8 are the basis of Christian doctrine. They are the systematic, intellectual unfolding of the foundational truths of the gospel of Jesus Christ.

- Chapters 9–11 are a kind of excursus, or fuller discussion, focusing on God's dealings with Israel. Included is an explanation of why, for a time, Israel has been set aside, as well as a statement of how Israel will again be reconciled to God in due course. So extraordinary was it that Israel was set aside for a time that Paul found it necessary to write three chapters of Romans explaining the situation.

- Chapters 12–16 essentially contain the practical outworking of the foundational truths covered in the previous chapters, helping us to apply these truths in our daily experiences and living. That is why verse 1 of chapter 12 begins with a *"therefore."* It begins in the light of all that was said in chapters 1–11.

In Romans 12:1–6, it is as if God is saying to us, "Now, here is your response." This is what He expects us to do:

I beseech you therefore, brethren, by the mercies of God, that you present your bodies a living sacrifice, holy, acceptable to God, which is your reasonable service. And do not be conformed to this world, but be transformed by the renewing of your mind, that you may prove what is that good and acceptable and perfect will of God. For I say, through the grace given to me, to everyone who is among you, not to think of himself more highly than he ought to think, but to think soberly, as God has dealt to each one a measure of faith. For as we have many members in one body, but all the members do not have the same function, so we, being many, are one body in Christ, and individually members of one another. Having then gifts differing according to the grace that is given to us, let us use them....

God Wants All of You

Paul unfolded a number of successive, logical steps in the above verses. In Romans 12:1, what is the first step God expects? That you present your body to Him.

Most people would try to begin with the spiritual, but God begins with the physical. He says, "I want your body—plus all it contains. I want the whole of you: spirit, soul, and body. Give Me the vessel, and I'll have the contents, as well."

In addition, God says, "I want your body placed on the altar as *'a living sacrifice.'*" This direction from God is a deliberate

contrast with the instructions concerning Old Testament sacrifices, where the animals were first killed and then placed on
the altar. God tells us, "I want you to put your body on My altar,
just as truly as those sacrificial beasts were placed on the altar under the Old Testament. And I want your body presented
to Me in exactly the same way that the sheep, oxen, and other
animals were presented on the altar, with this one exception: I
don't want you dead; I want you living." That is the only difference. Otherwise, the parallel is exact.

When Paul said we are to present our bodies as *"a living
sacrifice,...acceptable to God,"* he added, *"which is your reasonable service."* I believe that idea can be paraphrased, "It's the
least you can do in light of all that God has done for you. In light
of the truth of the gospel, it is the reasonable response." God
demands *you*—your body, your spirit, your mind, your talents,
all that you are and all that you have. What is your response?
You are to place it all on the altar.

The Altar Gives Value to the Sacrifice

For added insight regarding the altar, let's briefly examine
a beautiful illustration in Matthew 23. In this passage, Jesus
was rebuking the Jewish religious leaders for their foolish interpretations of Scripture. For one thing, they said that if you
swear by the altar in the temple, it doesn't matter; you don't
have to keep your oath. But if you swear by the sacrifice or the
gift that is placed *on* the altar, then you are bound to keep your
oath. Jesus reproved them, saying,

> *Fools and blind! For which is greater, the gift or the
> altar that sanctifies the gift?*   (Matthew 23:19)

Please notice that it isn't the gift that gives value to the
altar. It is the altar that gives value to the gift. The gift does
not sanctify the altar; the altar sanctifies the gift that is placed
upon it. Therefore, when you place your body upon the altar of

God, the altar sanctifies it. As long as you remain on the altar, you are sanctified by the altar. But please pay attention to this: If, at any time, you take your life off of God's altar, deciding to go your own way, to do your own thing, and to please yourself, you break contact with the altar. You lose your sanctification, because the altar sanctifies the gift that remains upon it.

You have to be grateful to God that He is willing to accept you. You are not doing God a favor by offering Him your life. God is doing you a favor by accepting your life. And He accepts it, not on the basis of what you are, but on the basis of the altar upon which you offer your life, which is *"Jesus Christ and Him crucified"* (1 Corinthians 2:2).

Renewing Your Mind

Next, we will look at Romans 12:2: *"And do not be conformed to this world, but be transformed by the renewing of your mind, that you may prove what is that good and acceptable and perfect will of God."* What happens when you place your body on the altar? You are renewed in your mind. Your way of thinking changes. Your mental attitudes, your ambitions, your relationships, your evaluations, and your standards are transformed. As all those factors are changed inwardly in your mind, your whole way of living changes. You are no longer conformed to the world, but you are transformed through this renewing of your mind.

> **When you place your body on the altar, your ambition, your relationships, and your standards are transformed.**

Let's examine the pattern of life in the world as presented in 1 John 2:15–17. Verses 15 and 16 describe the attitude of the carnal man. Then, verse 17 describes the spirit and attitude of the person who has been renewed in his mind through presenting his body on the altar.

> *Do not love the world or the things in the world. If anyone loves the world, the love of the Father is not in him. For all that is in the world; the lust of the flesh, the lust of the eyes, and the pride of life; is not of the Father but is of the world. And the world is passing away, and the lust of it; but he who does the will of God abides forever.* (1 John 2:15–17)

The carnal mind is taken up with *"the lust of the flesh, the lust of the eyes, and the pride of life."* It is taken up with things that are temporary—that do not abide, that are transient—things that have no real, permanent value. However, when you are renewed in your mind, and you begin to do the will of God as He has revealed it to your renewed mind, then you "abide forever."

Isn't that a beautiful Scripture? Why not take a moment to say that out loud? *"But he who does the will of God abides forever."*

I want to tell you something that will encourage you greatly. When you are doing God's will, you are unsinkable. You are irresistible. You are indestructible. Nothing can stand against you when you are doing the will of God.

How important it is, then, to find the will of God and to do it! How can you find the will of God? Present your body as a living sacrifice before God. When you present your body, your mind is renewed. Then, when your mind is renewed, you can find the will of God.

Finding the Will of God

The latter part of Romans 12:2 helps us to see some important aspects of the will of God:

...but be transformed by the renewing of your mind, that you may prove [find out in experience] *what is that good and acceptable and perfect will of God.*

(Romans 12:2)

Let's be honest. The old, unrenewed mind cannot find the will of God. Why? Because Paul said in Romans 8:7 that *"the carnal mind is enmity against God."* God simply will not reveal His will to the carnal mind. But when your mind has been renewed, it begins to find out in experience what the will of God is for your life.

> **When you come into perfect line with the will of God, every detail in your life is completely provided for.**

You discover God's will for you in three ascending phases: (1) good, (2) acceptable, and (3) perfect. When you come into perfect line with the will of God, every detail in your life is completely provided for. Not the slightest detail is omitted in God's perfect will. However, it takes the renewing of your mind to find God's will. And, as you move into God's will, you do not necessarily move immediately into the perfection of His will. At first, it is good; then, it is acceptable; but, in the fulfillment, it is perfect.

Walking in Your Measure of Faith

Romans 12:3 gives us the next step after we have discovered the will of God:

For I say, through the grace given to me, to everyone who is among you, not to think of himself more highly than he ought to think, but to think soberly [humbly, realistically], *as God has dealt to each one a measure* [proportion] *of faith.*

God has given you the measure of faith needed to do His will. Bear in mind that God has not given you the measure of faith needed to do something other than His will for you. As soon as you have found the will of God, there is a balance between God's will and your faith. If a person is always struggling for faith to accomplish his or her pursuit, that is almost sure proof that such a person is not walking in the will of God. This Scripture makes it clear that when you have found the will of God, your first realization is that God has already deposited in you a measure of faith that is equal to the task He wants you to perform.

Many years ago, my first wife, Lydia, moved to Jerusalem, Israel, without any support. She left a good home and a secure job in Denmark. Once in Israel, Lydia started taking in little unwanted girls. In all, she brought up about seventy children over a number of years—with practically no money. When she took in the first baby girl, Lydia had about six dollars in her purse. She had no crib and no bedding. She simply opened her wicker trunk, lined it with soft articles of clothing, wrapped the little girl in a woolen sweater, and laid her in the trunk—and that is how Lydia started a children's home. Many were the nights that she would stay up praying to receive the children's breakfast for the next morning.

When Lydia and I began planning to get married, I thought to myself, *I'm not sure that I'm equal to that kind of life. I really don't know that I have that kind of faith.* I remember that the Lord spoke so sweetly to me in answer to my concern, saying, "You don't need that kind of faith, because I haven't asked you to live that kind of life. I've given you the faith for what I want you to do."

Lydia often said to me in the years after we were married, "I couldn't do it today." Why not? Because God wasn't asking her to do it at that time in her life. What God asks you to do, He gives you the faith to do. But God does not give you the faith to do something He has not asked you to do.

If there is a continual conflict between your faith and what you are trying to do, please be aware, my dear friend, that you may be trying to do the wrong thing. Possibly, you have not found the will of God. And the reason may be that you have not been renewed in your mind. If that is the case, you have not yet put your body on the altar.

Being a Member of the Body of Christ

In verses 4 and 5 of Romans 12, we take the next step after recognizing our measure of faith:

For as we have many members in one body, but all the members do not have the same function, so we, being many, are one body in Christ, and individually members of one another.

Your next discovery is that you are a member of the body of Christ. You have a particular place and a specific function. It is essential to discover your position in the body. There is only one place where you can function properly, and that is the place where God has ordained you to be. If God has made you a "hand," you will be a miserable failure if you try to play the part of a "foot." If God has made you an "eye," you will never function well as an "ear." (See 1 Corinthians 12:14–27.) You have to find your place in the body. When you discover what member you are, then you will function without effort—relaxed, free, and unembarrassed.

My hand has no problem being a hand. It "enjoys" being a hand. It can do all the things a hand should do. But if I tell my hand, "Now, you should be a foot. Put on a shoe and try to walk," there will be no end to the problems. Unfortunately, there are a lot of hands trying to be feet in the body of Christ at the present time. There are many eyes trying to be ears. The reason for this situation is that people have not followed the steps laid down in the Word to find their places in the body.

Exercising Your Gift

The final truth we will look at from Romans 12 is in verse 6: *"Having then gifts differing according to the grace that is given to us, let us use them...."* This is the point where gifts come in—not at the beginning, but at the end of the line. When you have found your place, when you are doing your job, when you are fulfilling your function, do you know what you will discover? You will find that the gifts you need are there to do the job.

> **When you are fulfilling your function, you will find that the gifts you need are there to do the job.**

Please don't pray arbitrarily, "Lord, I want the gift of prophecy," or "I want gifts of healings," or "I want the gift of interpretation." That is not the way to pray. Rather, pray in this way: "Lord, show me my place in the body of Christ. Show me what You want me to do."

I tell you truthfully, you will hardly have to pray for gifts when you find your place and start to do your job. You will discover, to your surprise, that the gifts will come into operation.

When I got into the ministry of deliverance, two spiritual gifts began to operate in me without my even planning on them. One was the discerning of spirits, and the other was the word of knowledge. (See 1 Corinthians 12:7–10.) I remember an early effort to minister deliverance to a lady in Denver, Colorado, in 1964. There were several people praying in the room, and I sat down beside her on a sofa. She looked at me in a helpless, pitiful way, and I felt real compassion in my heart. To my surprise, I said, "You need deliverance from..." and I listed about fifteen spirits. I thought to myself, *Where did that come from? How did I know that?* Immediately, I realized that it must have been the word of knowledge.

I did not have to agonize for five days in fasting and prayer, saying, "Lord, give me the word of knowledge." I had come to the place where I needed the word of knowledge to do the will of God. And God saw to it that I was given the word of knowledge. That is the correct order.

The Divine, Logical Order

From all that we have discussed in this chapter, let's briefly review the steps of our response to God's choice, as outlined in Romans 12:1–6:

1. You present your body on God's altar (Jesus Christ, and Him crucified). If you have never taken that step, I am going to give you an opportunity to do so at the end of this book. You should know for sure if you have done it. If you are not sure, you probably have not yet taken that step.

2. When you present your body on God's altar, you are then renewed in your mind. You begin to think in entirely different ways. In thinking differently, you live differently. You are no longer conformed to the world. You are transformed in your behavior.

3. God's will for you is then revealed to your renewed mind. You discover God's will progressively in three distinct stages: good, acceptable, and perfect.

4. As you discover God's will, you find that you have the faith needed to do His will. God has given you the proportionate faith required to do what He is asking you to do.

5. As you discover God's will, you find your place and particular function in the body of Christ. You discover what "member" you are and how you are to operate.

6. As you learn your place and begin to fulfill your function in it, you find yourself exercising the needed gifts.

This is the divine, logical order when you are a living sacrifice. It is your proper response to God's choice. Again, Jesus said, *"You did not choose Me, but I chose you"* (John 15:16). When you realize that God has chosen you, then you will make the kind of response we have talked about in this chapter.

20

SHAPING YOUR LIFE

From what you have read in the previous chapter, you are undoubtedly aware that changes will be coming to your life. As God's will is progressively revealed to you, you will progressively shape your whole life and conduct to fulfill it. This is clear direction toward the ultimate purpose of your life. This is what makes sanctification meaningful.

To accomplish this transformation by which you begin to fulfill your purpose and partake of the divine nature, you will need to become very much like an athlete in training. In that regard, I want to look at two statements of the apostle Paul. I'll begin with Acts 24:16, one of my favorite verses:

> *And herein do I exercise myself, to have always a conscience void of offence toward God, and toward men.*
>
> (KJV)

Finding and maintaining the state Paul described requires spiritual exercise, as he stated in the opening words of this verse. It requires application.

Next, let's look at 1 Corinthians 9, where Paul deliberately applied to himself as a minister of Christ the examples and principles drawn from the experiences of athletic contestants.

> *Do you not know that those who run in a race all run, but one receives the prize? Run in such a way that you may obtain it. And everyone who competes for the prize is temperate in all things.*   (verses 24–25)

Any person who wants to succeed in athletics has to put himself under a strict, disciplined regimen.

> *Now they do it to obtain a perishable crown, but we for an imperishable crown.* (1 Corinthians 9:25)

Athletes compete for perishable crowns, such as gold, silver, or bronze Olympic medals, but we discipline ourselves spiritually for an eternal medal, a *"crown of glory that does not fade away"* (1 Peter 5:4).

Paul continued,

> *Therefore I run thus: not with uncertainty.*
> (1 Corinthians 9:26)

He was saying, "I know where I'm headed. I don't wander from side to side on the track; I don't roam from lane to lane. I've got a mark, and I'm pressing toward it."

> *Thus I fight: not as one who beats the air.* (verse 26)

In other words, "When I encounter the devil and his forces, I aim my blows to hit where it hurts most. I don't just lash out wildly with my fists and hope that a blow will land on them."

> *But I discipline my body and bring it into subjection, lest, when I have preached to others, I myself should become disqualified.* (verse 27)

Note Paul's emphasis on the body again. You must not despise and belittle your physical body. Your body is the vessel of your spirit and your mind. It is a dwelling place, or temple, of the Holy Spirit. (See 1 Corinthians 3:16; 6:19.) You have an obligation to keep that temple in the best possible order. You are duty-bound to keep it holy, not defiling it with unclean or excessive habits of any kind. You are not to indulge in gluttony or any other practice that defiles and weakens the temple of God.

> **You are duty-bound to keep your body holy, not defiling it with unclean or excessive habits.**

Paul said, in effect, "I treat my body like an athlete treats his body. I keep it under subjection. I don't let it dictate to me." Let me make this pointed statement: The body is a good servant but a fearful master. Never let your body master you. Master your body.

In relation to this, I like the words of my good friend Don Basham, who once said, "My stomach doesn't tell me when to eat; I tell my stomach when to eat." That is the point. Don't let your body dictate to you. Our bodies are wonderful creations. All of us can say with David, *"I am fearfully and wonderfully made"* (Psalm 139:14). Therefore, we should never despise the body. The body is not evil. It is good. Treat it that way. Preserve it. And dedicate it to fulfilling the task.

Disciplined Response

Let's look more closely at the pattern of the athlete who sets himself to succeed in a contest. His goal is to jump higher, swim faster, run more swiftly, or do whatever else he needs to accomplish. How does he do that? He applies himself in two ways: exercise and discipline. We need to recognize these as essential parts of Christian living, as well. An athlete renounces all that hinders the accomplishment of his special aim. He cultivates all that helps it.

I have been a part of the Pentecostal movement ever since I became a Christian. Yet one problem with the Pentecostal movement was that people got so excited about the gifts of the Spirit that they no longer paid attention to the need for the fruit of the Spirit and for spiritual discipline. And gifts are no substitute for fruit.

Jesus said, *"You will know them by their fruits"* (Matthew 7:16)—not by their gifts. In fact, Jesus rebuked people who were practicing lawlessness and yet exercising spiritual gifts. (See verses 21–23.) There are such people in the world today. They practice lawlessness, they make their own rules, they set their own standards, they are submitted to nobody, and they are exercising spiritual gifts.

This is possible because, when God gives a gift, He never withdraws it. The gifts are not conditional loans. They are outright gifts, and we are responsible for the use we make of them. We can do one of three things: (1) we can use them properly; (2) we can fail to use them and, therefore, lose them; or, (3) we can misuse them. But they are still ours, and we are accountable to God for what we do with them.

You see, we have come back to the beginning of sanctification. When I set myself to do the will of God, I put my body on the altar. When I place myself there as a living sacrifice, my mind is renewed, and I discover the will of God. Then, I set my goal. I discipline my whole being to do God's will. For what purpose? For the purpose of revealing and glorifying the Lord Jesus Christ, the One who chose me, the One who sanctified me, the One who sent me.

Do you want to reveal Jesus? Do you want to glorify Him? You accomplish that only in the way Jesus revealed and glorified the Father. You accomplish it by finding and doing the Father's will.

Are You Satisfied?

God spoke to me very clearly a number of years ago, and He challenged me directly. I had come to a certain level in my Christian experience, and, at that point, He asked, "Are you satisfied? Or do you want to go further?" God forgive me, but do you know what I said? "Lord, *if there is anything further*, I want to go further." After all, I was a successful Pentecostal preacher! I had served Him selflessly as a missionary. I am sure God was aware of all that when He asked me, "Are you satisfied? Or do you want to go further?"

Honestly, I am embarrassed that my first thought was, *Well, Lord, what could be further?* But when God asked me that, I responded, "Lord, if there is anything further, I want to go further."

Then the Lord answered me very clearly, saying, "There are two conditions. First of all, all progress in the Christian life is by faith. If you are not willing to go forward in faith, you cannot go forward. Second, if you are to fulfill the ministry that I have for you, you will need a strong, healthy body. And you're putting on too much weight. You had better see to that."

It was very timely advice, and I was grateful to receive it. I think it saved me a lot of money in doctor bills in the ensuing years. The point I want to make, though, is that God showed me my body was an integral part of His plan for my life. If I did not keep my body in the order that He required, I could not fulfill His plan.

Please remember that although you are made up of spirit, soul, and body, you are not three different pieces floating about, loosely linked together. You are a unit. The body is the vessel that contains the spirit and the soul. Do you recall what I wrote earlier about God saying, "Give Me the vessel, and I'll have the contents, as well"? Don't try to give Him a "disembodied" spirit or soul. He is not asking for that. He is asking for your body on His altar. Preserve your body. Discipline your body. Dedicate the members of your body to Him. Yield your members to God as instruments of righteousness.

Supernatural Help

I would like to challenge you right now. I promised God long ago that I would never again give just a religious lecture but always provide an opportunity for my listeners and readers to respond to the message that I presented.

Right now, my challenge is clear: Are you willing to present your body as a living sacrifice?

If you want to respond to that challenge in a positive way, the best step is to commit yourself to the Lord in prayer. Here is a prayer you can use to do just that:

> Father, I come to You in the name of Jesus, and I present myself to You. I place myself as a living sacrifice on Your altar. I declare that You are holy and that there is no one like You in all the universe. You are a holy God, and I bow before You, acknowledging Your absolute righteousness and holiness, and Your absolute right to my life.
>
> Father, because You are holy, You have commanded that Your people are to be holy, as well. I readily confess that I cannot walk in holiness by my own power or strength. Even my best efforts and works do not qualify. So, I throw myself completely upon Your mercy and grace.
>
> Help me, Father, to walk in holiness and obedience before You, even as Your holy Son, Jesus, did. Empower me by Your Holy Spirit to live in a way that is pleasing to You. Father, I commit my entire life to You now. In Jesus' name, amen.

By praying that prayer, you have taken a very important step in following the Lord completely in a life of holiness. Periodically, you will need to pray this prayer again, because the simple truth is that there will come times when you will miss the mark and fall short.

At those times, just remember that our God is a loving Father, and that Jesus our Savior, who knows what it is like to be human, is interceding for us even now. (See Hebrews 7:25.) We also have Jesus' assurance that our Helper, the Holy Spirit, will lead us and guide us into all truth (see John 16:13), reminding

> **Jesus knows what it is like to be human, and He is interceding for us even now.**

us always of all that Jesus did and taught (see John 14:26).

With that kind of supernatural help, you will be able to succeed in walking before the Lord in holiness and obedience. May He help you in every way. May He empower you through the words you have read in this book. And may He bless you and bring you fulfillment as you set yourself apart for Him and His purposes.

ABOUT THE AUTHOR

Derek Prince (1915–2003) was born in India of British parents. He was educated as a scholar of Greek and Latin at Eton College and King's College, Cambridge, in England. Upon graduation, he held a fellowship (equivalent to a professorship) in Ancient and Modern Philosophy at King's College. Prince also studied Hebrew, Aramaic, and modern languages at Cambridge and the Hebrew University in Jerusalem. As a student, he was a philosopher and self-proclaimed agnostic.

While in the British Medical Corps during World War II, Prince began to study the Bible as a philosophical work. Converted through a powerful encounter with Jesus Christ, he was baptized in the Holy Spirit a few days later. Out of this encounter, he formed two conclusions: first, that Jesus Christ is alive; second, that the Bible is a true, relevant, up-to-date book. These conclusions altered the whole course of his life, which he then devoted to studying and teaching the Bible as the Word of God.

Discharged from the army in Jerusalem in 1945, he married Lydia Christensen, founder of a children's home there. Upon their marriage, he immediately became father to Lydia's eight adopted daughters—six Jewish, one Palestinian Arab, and one English. Together, the family saw the rebirth of the state of Israel in 1948. In the late 1950s, they adopted another daughter while Prince was serving as principal of a teacher training college in Kenya.

In 1963, the Princes immigrated to the United States and pastored a church in Seattle. In 1973, Prince became one of the founders of Intercessors for America. His book *Shaping History through Prayer and Fasting* has awakened Christians around the world to their responsibility to pray for their governments. Many consider underground translations of the book as instrumental in the fall of communist regimes in the USSR, East Germany, and Czechoslovakia.

Lydia Prince died in 1975, and Prince married Ruth Baker (a single mother to three adopted children) in 1978. He met his second wife, like his first wife, while she was serving the Lord in Jerusalem. Ruth died in December 1998 in Jerusalem, where they had lived since 1981.

Until a few years before his own death in 2003 at the age of eighty-eight, Prince persisted in the ministry God had called him to as he traveled the world, imparting God's revealed truth, praying for the sick and afflicted, and sharing his prophetic insights into world events in the light of Scripture. Internationally recognized as a Bible scholar and spiritual patriarch, Derek Prince established a teaching ministry that spanned six continents and more than sixty years. He is the author of more than fifty books, six hundred audio teachings, and one hundred video teachings, many of which have been translated and published in more than one hundred languages. He pioneered teaching on such groundbreaking themes as generational curses, the biblical significance of Israel, and demonology.

Prince's radio program, which began in 1979, has been translated into more than a dozen languages and continues to touch lives. Derek's main gift of explaining the Bible and its teaching in a clear and simple way has helped build a foundation of faith in millions of lives. His nondenominational, nonsectarian approach has made his teaching equally relevant and helpful to people from all racial and religious backgrounds, and his teaching is estimated to have reached more than half the globe.

In 2002, he said, "It is my desire—and I believe the Lord's desire—that this ministry continue the work, which God began through me over sixty years ago, until Jesus returns."

Derek Prince Ministries International continues to reach out to believers in over 140 countries with Derek's teaching, fulfilling the mandate to keep on "until Jesus returns." This is accomplished through the outreaches of more than thirty Derek Prince offices around the world, including primary work in Australia, Canada, China, France, Germany, the Netherlands, New Zealand, Norway, Russia, South Africa, Switzerland, the United Kingdom, and the United States. For current information about these and other worldwide locations, visit www.derekprince.org.